JOHN BAILEY'S FISHING GUIDES

WHERE TO
SEA
F|SH
IN BRITAIN
& IRELAND

JOHN BAILEY'S FISHING GUIDES

WHERE TO
SEA
F|SH
IN BRITAIN
& IRELAND

John Bailey

NEW HOLLAND

First published in 2003 by New Holland Publishers (UK) Ltd
London • Cape Town • Sydney • Auckland

www.newhollandpublishers.com

2 4 6 8 10 9 7 5 3 1

Garfield House, 86–88 Edgware Road, London W2 2EA

80 McKenzie Street, Cape Town 8001, South Africa

14 Aquatic Drive, Frenchs Forest, NSW 2086, Australia

218 Lake Road, Northcote, Auckland, New Zealand

ISBN 1 84330 010 9

Edited and designed by Design Revolution Limited,
Queens Park Villa, 30 West Drive, Brighton BN2 0QW
Project Editor: Ian Whitelaw
Designer: Andrew Easton
Editor: Julie Whitaker

Index by Indexing Specialists,
202 Church Road, Hove BN3 2DJ

Publishing Manager: Jo Hemmings
Senior Editor: Kate Michell
Assistant Editor: Anne Konopelski
Production Controller: Joan Woodroffe

Reproduction by Pica Digital Pte Ltd, Singapore
Printed and bound in Singapore by Kyodo Printing Co
(Singapore) Pte Ltd

CONTENTS

INTRODUCTION

We hear a great deal about the rape of the seas in the press and on the television. One would think that the oceans are barren places, totally stripped of fish by rapacious trawler fleets. Well, quite obviously, there is some truth in these reports, and stocks of some fish, cod especially, are certainly far less than they were some years back. But, thankfully, this is not the complete picture and the whole truth is somewhat more hopeful.

I've been researching this present book for some two and a half years and, during that time, I've spoken to innamerable sea anglers from every part of the United Kingdom. Okay, there have been some laments for times past but, on the whole, there is a healthy optimism, and certainly great praise for the wealth and variety of fishing that there is to be enjoyed around our spectacular coastline.

One interesting side-effect of global warming appears to be a wider variety of fish visiting our shores. In this book, for example, you'll read about the possibilities of tuna off the Irish coast and, only recently, I have heard rumours of sailfish off the Lincolnshire coast. Another angler has heard of a barracuda caught in an offshore net... the last barracuda I hooked was in the Bahamas! Who knows, could it be bonefish taking your fly in a shallow Devonshire cove next summer!?

Fish native to our home waters also seem to be on the increase. Bass are a good example – not only are numbers apparently increasing in their well-known hotspots, but they are also appearing in good numbers along stretches of coast that previously scarcely had a bass run at all. Indeed, anglers in North Yorkshire are beginning to pick up this stunning species with some regularity.

Not long ago, I was chatting to a guy who has a boat off the Cumbrian coast, and he was telling me of the glorious summer and autumn he'd had fishing poppers just off the rocky headlands thereabouts. It seemed that he needed to get into his boat and cast in to the shore for guaranteed success. Fishing from the rocks out to sea did little good at all. Strangely, this is a situation I've found mirrored exactly along my home coast here in north Norfolk.

Sea trout also appear to be making some sort of recovery after a worrying absence in many areas. Moreover, they are beginning to make regular appearances in areas you wouldn't expect to find them. Sussex, for example, is reporting more and more of this glamorous species. And mullet once again appear to be visiting our shores in ever-increasing numbers during the summer, and, yet again, there is hardly any estuary, harbour or marshland dyke where you can't expect to find a run at some time or another.

More sea anglers are now moving into the sporting arena. If we look back, certainly to my childhood, the majority of sea anglers probably went out with rod, reel and newspaper pack of worms in order to augment the family's food supply. Nothing wrong in that. But a growing number of sea anglers are now beginning to realise that genuine sport can be had from the sea – and not just the ritual laughter of comparatively small fish on hugely heavy tackle! Rods and reels have become lighter over the decades and more fun to use. Lines have improved vastly, especially the stronger ones that used to kink as uncontrollably as coiled wire. Boats are faster and cleaner. Methods have also improved and there's now a wealth of material and advice that simply wasn't present before.

Moreover, we can all get to the seaside much more easily now than half a century ago. Those who lived inland were likely to have just one sea-fishing outing during the course of a year. Generally, that was aboard some wheezing charabanc that would crawl its way from a northern industrial town sometime before dawn on a winter Sunday. Chances are, too, that you'd spend most of the day seasick and miserable and, in short, your freedom for manoeuvre and experimentation was pretty well limited. Today, fast roads mean that you can get to the coast in a fraction of the time. More people, too, have the money to hire a skipper. There's also better bait available and a whole host of new ideas.

We have a magnificently varied shoreline. For example, I generally fish the comparatively gentle Norfolk coastline. It might not be heart-stopping, but it has its own fascination, especially on a misty, summer dawn when the bass are scattering the small fry. But that doesn't mean I don't go up to Scotland and enjoy the magnificent craggy, coastline of the Isles. And then there is Ireland, which has hundreds of miles of almost virgin shoreline to offer. And what about Devon and Cornwall, or the grandeur of Wales or the Lake District? And I haven't even mentioned the south coast, where you can catch virtually every sea fish that swims.

What I'm hoping is that this small book will find a nesting place in your car glove compartment where it can serve its purpose once or twice a year when you are away from home. I doubt whether I'm passing on anything that the local expert won't know, but I hope I'm offering signposts to the thousands of anglers who like to travel and face fresh challenges.

I'd be irresponsible, though, if I didn't offer a few cautionary words. Always enlist local advice when it comes to the best access and exit and, especially, any potential problems with rising tides or threatening winds. If you are a boat angler, check conditions thoroughly before setting out, and always ensure that people know where you are going and what time you will return. And always act as an ambassador for our sport. Remember your sportsmanship and clear away your own litter and any other litter you might find. Let's keep our seas and beaches as pristine as possible.

Scale

mls 0 10 20 30 40 50 60 70 80 90 100
kms 0 20 40 60 80 100

FAROE
ISLANDS

SHETLANDS

ORKNEY

SCOTLAND

GLASGOW EDINBURGH

LONDONDERRY

BELFAST

IRELAND

NORTH
WEST

NORTH EAST

NEWCASTLE UPON TYNE
SUNDERLAND

DUBLIN

BRADFORD LEEDS HULL
MANCHESTER
LIVERPOOL SHEFFIELD

STOKE-ON-TRENT

LIMERICK

DERBY NOTTINGHAM

WOLVERHAMPTON LEICESTER

WATERFORD

BIRMINGHAM COVENTRY

LINCOLNSHIRE
TO ESSEX

CORK

WALES

CARDIFF BRISTOL

LONDON

HAMPSHIRE
AND
DORSET

SOUTH
EAST

SOUTH
WEST

SOUTHAMPTON

PLYMOUTH

N

JERSEY

Sea-Fishing Sites from Lincolnshire to Essex

Louth
Mablethorpe
LEICESTERSHIRE
A153
A157
A16
A52
A1028
Ingoldmells
A158
Skegness
A16
A52
Boston
A52
Hunstanton
A16
A17
The Wash
A151
Holbeach
A17
Brancaster
Wells-next-the-Sea
Blakeney Point
Salthouse
Sheringham
Cromer
Overstrand
A149
Cley next the Sea
Weybourne
Trimingham
Mundesley
A148
Bacton
Happisburg
Sea Palling
King's Lynn
Fakenham
A148
A47
NORFOLK
North Walsham
Horsey
A1062
Dereham
A47
A140
A1151
Winterton-on-Sea
Hemsby
Wisbech
A10
A47
Swaffham
Norwich
A47
Caister-on-Sea
Downham Market
A47
A146
A143
Great Yarmouth
March
A1101
A10
A11
Gorleston on Sea
Hopton on Sea
Lowestoft
A134
Chatteris
Ely
Thetford
A1066
A140
A143
Beccles
A144
A145
Kessingland
CAMBRIDGESHIRE
Huntingdon
St Ives
A11
Mildenhall
A143
Halesworth
Southwold
Blythe Water
A14
Bury St Edmunds
SUFFOLK
A12
Newmarket
A14
A140
Aldeburgh
A428
Cambridge
A134
Stowmarket
River Deben
Aldeburgh Bay
Orford
Orford Ness
Woodbridge
M11
A14
A10
Haverhill
Sudbury
Ipswich
Hollesley Bay
Royston
Saffron Walden
A12
Shotley
Felixstowe
Manningtree
Harwich
Dovercourt
A131
The Naze
Walton on the Naze
Braintree
A120
A120
Frinton-on-Sea
A130
Colchester
A133
Clacton-on-Sea
M11
A12
Witham
West Mersea
ESSEX
A12
Chelmsford
A414
Maldon
Brentwood
A12
A130
Burnham-on-Crouch
Foulness Island
Basildon
Southend-on-Sea
A13
Canvey Island
Tilbury

N

■ Foreshore
■ Sand bank

30m

I've known this coastline all my life. I was brought up here, and my whole life is concerned with conservation on the marshes at Cley. Okay, this east coast doesn't have the dramatic cliffs and huge surf of, say, Cornwall, but there's a quiet mystery and charm about it all. You should see it on a summer evening when the sea is molten and the marshes are on fire. Or during a winter storm when there's a gale blowing down from the north and nothing separating us from the Pole. It's a seashore of mists and seeping tides, and you've got to watch out for potential dangers. The fishing is thrilling. Obviously, there are those who say it's not as good as it once was, but it's still good enough for me and plenty of others. Perhaps the big cod aren't here in the numbers that they once were, but there are lots of other things to keep you occupied. Fishing for flatfish is as good as ever, and the bass fishing is certainly on the way up. Of course, we also have our secrets – it's not unusual to catch the odd sea trout, and we get great invasions of mullet during the summer.

BERNARD BISHOP, NORFOLK WILDLIFE TRUST WARDEN FOR CLEY MARSHES

Bernard is quite correct. The east coast of England and dramatic sea fishing aren't always seen to go entirely hand-in-hand, but this is certainly a big mistake. The bass fishing in most areas can be absolutely superb – from spring right through to the early days of winter. Moreover, it seems that there are more and more bass appearing every summer, and the winter fishing for codling and whiting can, at times, be excellent. If you have access to a boat, then you can expect worthwhile skate fishing in places, and even the possibility of some good tope. There was a time when the Wash was considered one of the very best areas for these fabulous fish, and the rumour is that they're on their way back. Hopefully, conservation will ensure their long-term survival.

LINCOLNSHIRE TO ESSEX

MABLETHORPE

The area from Mablethorpe south to Skegness comprises miles of flat, sandy beaches. These beaches are very shallow and open to the winds, which doesn't make them particularly conducive to boat fishing. However, the beach fishing can be extraordinarily good. Mablethorpe is busy throughout the summer months when the tourists descend, but it dies a death during the winter, and the anglers come into their own.

Try the amusement park end of the beach and around the Trustville holiday camp. You will find that the beaches are clean and that they fish particularly well at low water. Worm is a favourite bait, but crab produces good catches of flounder.

Moving south, Chapel St Leonards, Chapel Point, Six Marshes, Nearby Creek, Mogs Eye and Huttoft are all popular fishing spots. The whole area can be very good for summer bass. Try lug – especially black lug – and don't make the mistake of trying to cast out too far.

You won't find any charter boats in this area, but the dinghy fishing can be very good for bass, eels and flatfish. There are thornbacks around, but you will have to go quite a few miles offshore to find these.

ACCOMMODATION – the Tourist Information Centre in Mablethorpe on 01507 472496 can advise on accommodation in the area.

TACKLE SHOPS – it's a good idea to have a word with the tackle shop in St Leonards, which is an absolute gold-mine of information; call Chapel Tackle on 01754 871657.

SKEGNESS

Skegness isn't quite the magnet it used to be, since its famous long pier sank to a watery grave nearly quarter of a century ago, destroyed by gales and floods. There are still a few anglers that fish around this historic spot, but most of the locals move slightly further along the beach to Ingoldmells.

The Butlins holiday camp is a well-known mark, both winter and summer. The bass fishing can be very good, but also expect smooth-hounds and dogfish to feature. Crab is a winning bait. Come winter, there are plenty of codling and whiting about, with some big cod, well into double figures, occasionally showing up. Lugworm, fished on an incoming tide, is hard to beat. At high tide, cast shorter.

ACCOMMODATION – this is an area with plenty of hotels. For details, contact the Tourist Information Centre in Skegness on 01754 764821.

TACKLE SHOPS – contact Skegness Fishing Tackle on 01754 764404 for up-to-the-minute angling information.

THE WASH AND THE OUSE ESTUARY

The Wash can be featureless in places, but the Great Ouse River offers some tremendous possibilities. It flows northwards into the bottom right-hand side of the Wash at King's Lynn. You can find fishing within the town itself, as well as on the outskirts. What is also appealing about the place is that it's very much under-fished, and you're certainly unlikely to be struggling for bank space.

The Ouse Estuary was tremendously popular back in the 1950s and 1960s, when locals pioneered fly fishing for both bass and mullet. You'll be very unlikely to see anybody wielding a fly rod in the area these days, but the bass seem to exist in ever-increasing numbers. Basically, the bass move in from April, and you'll find mullet from May until September. You can also expect large catches of eels and flounder, and even the occasional sole. This is a perfect area for the exploring angler and one who is, perhaps, on holiday close by on the Norfolk coast – say at Hunstanton or Heacham.

Those that fish the area swear by peeler crabs, although bread can work for the mullet, and even maggots and garden worms do well at times. Obviously, standard beach gear will do the job, but you'll get far more out of your sport if you fish a little bit lighter. For example, try light spinning for the bass and coarse float tackle for the mullet. You'll even find that you catch far more eels on a five- or six-pound line, which is quite up to the job.

ACCOMMODATION – call Hunstanton Tourist Information Centre on 01485 532610.

TACKLE SHOPS – in King's Lynn, contact either the Tackle Box on 01553 761293 or Anglers' Corner on 01553 775852 for detailed information, bait or tackle.

CLEY TO CROMER

The long pebble beach between Cley next the Sea and Weybourne has long been a favourite area for local anglers pursuing bass and flatfish in the summer, and cod, codling and whiting throughout the winter.

There's easy access from the main A149 coast road down to these beaches, and there is convenient parking. However, it often pays to walk a little way from the main crowd – for example towards Weybourne cliffs, which have a great reputation for producing the bigger bass.

Sheringham is building up a good angling reputation, especially since the flood defences were erected at the centre of the town beach. You'll find abundant bass here, with a good number of spring cod. Flatfish are present all year, and there are plenty of mackerel between June and September.

Be careful at the main beaches, which are crowded throughout the holiday season. The same goes for Cromer. In the height of the summer,

13

it's probably best to fish early or late and/or off the pier, which you can access for a small charge. You'll pick up occasional mackerel from the end of the pier and perhaps even the odd tope in the summer. There are also good skate and bass around.

⊨ ACCOMMODATION – for details of accommodation in the area, phone the Tourist Information Centres in Cromer on 01263 512497 or Sheringham on 01263 824329. Alternatively, try the George Hotel in Cley next the Sea on 01263 740652. Also highly recommended is the Dunn Cow – a small, family-run pub in Salthouse that offers excellent accommodation; phone them on 01263 740467.

○ TACKLE SHOPS – the Angling Direct shop in Cromer on 01263 513676 is the hub of sea fishing in this area and will offer you good advice.

OVERSTRAND, TRIMINGHAM AND MUNDESLEY

Continuing south east, Overstrand and Trimingham offer good possibilities for codling, occasional bass and flounder. If you're fishing the promenade at Overstrand, long casting frequently pays dividends.

Mundesley is a charming little holiday town that offers some interesting fishing, too. The beaches are sandy, with odd patches of shingle and stone. There are gullies and sandbanks that dry out on large, low tides. You'll find the water shallow and very difficult to fish during rough seas.

The most productive time, locals agree, is three hours before high tide and two hours down. It's best to fish the gullies between the sandbanks and the shore – anywhere between fifty and 150 yards from the high-tide mark. You'll pick up good dabs and flounder, cod in winter and spring, and the odd bass and sole during the summer. Watch out for whiting once autumn comes. Mundesley is easily reached on the B1159 south of Cromer, and there are plenty of signs to the beach.

⊨ ACCOMMODATION – for various kinds of accommodation available in the area, contact the Tourist Information Centre in Mundesley on 01263 721070.

○ TACKLE SHOPS – the best is the Angling Direct shop in Cromer on 01263 513676.

BACTON, HAPPISBURGH, SEA PALLING AND WINTERTON-ON-SEA

All these locations further down the north-east coast of Norfolk offer good chances of some really good bass throughout the summer period

The shingle bank from Blakeney Point down past the beaches at Cley next the Sea and Salthouse can, at times, provide some of the most stunning angling action imaginable. This is a very beautiful area, and a great favourite for holiday-makers drawn to the quaint Norfolk coastline, with its attractive little villages tucked away behind the marshes. The marshes themselves represent some of the most sought-after bird-watching territory in the United Kingdom.

The bass seem to come in quite early in the year, but the peak period is from June right through to October. One problem for anglers is the lack of real fish-holding features along this part of the shore. There are the occasional spots that are well known to the locals, but the casual visitor is advised to keep as mobile as possible. For this reason, it's a good idea to try spinning, especially when the sea is comparatively clear and weed isn't too much of a problem. You need something big and flashy – a big silver spoon isn't a bad option, providing you work it quickly so that it doesn't sink and foul the bottom. Above all, experiment. For example, on really calm days when you can see the bass splashing at the top, a 'popper' plug is worth trying; it's almost like American-style fishing for freshwater bass.

The bass do shoal quite tightly – I was talking to a local angler a few months ago who had managed to land eighty in one afternoon, admittedly from his small boat, but he was only some twenty yards out from the beach. I'm glad to say that he put back all but half a dozen. The fish were between two and seven pounds, about average for this area.

So, if you fancy some thrilling bass fishing in a wonderful, wild environment, then this could be just the place for you.

There's great accommodation around, too – Cley Mill Guesthouse is particularly in demand, with its wonderful views over the marsh. Phone 01263 740209 for details.

The angling shop in Cromer, Angling Direct (formerly known as Marine Sports), offers the most up-to-the-minute advice. Phone them on 01263 513676.

Lugworm can be bought locally from the many villages – simply look for the signs outside the houses. Lugworm can prove a very good alternative to the spinner. Simply use light gear, a weight just heavy enough to hold bottom, and feel for bites. You needn't cast far out – twenty yards is often far enough – and you can be in for a thrilling time if you locate the fish.

LUGWORM DIGGING

Given the price of worms sold commercially, it makes good sense to get out there on the beaches and dig your own. The following tips may help:

• *Always check that digging on a particular beach is permitted as there are many restricted areas.*

• *Always ensure that you are down on the grounds at low water and leave well before the incoming tide.*

• *Never take any risks with the weather. If it looks as though it's going to be stormy, then don't go out.*

• *Never go far from the shore, especially in mist or foggy conditions as it's easy to become disoriented. If you're in any doubt, take a compass.*

• *As far as equipment is concerned, you'll need good thigh boots, a strong wide-pronged fork, and a net and a bucket to wash your worms. A good warm coat can be vital to keep out a piercing wind.*

• *Look for a dry area with many worm casts. Dig a trench some five yards long and then go back to the head and keep turning over in a rhythmical, methodical manner.*

• *Once your trench begins to flood seriously, turning the sand into liquid ooze, then it's time to pull out and look for another area to work.*

• *During cold weather, the worms will go deeper and you'll need to go down more than the normal eighteen inches or so.*

• *Don't rush your digging – you'll only tire yourself out and achieve lower numbers. Give yourself frequent rests to let your back have a breather.*

• *Watch your hands for emerging blisters. These can be very painful, especially if they crack and get sand and salt in them. It's a good idea to wear mitts with the fingers removed. (In my professional digging days, I once found myself putting thirty-two bits of plaster on my hands and fingers on a Saturday evening!)*

• *Ignore worms that you've broken. Leave them for the seabirds because they will only die and infect the rest in your bucket.*

• *Don't take immature worms and don't dig too high up on the marsh where the small worms create their nurseries. Move towards the sea where the worms are larger.*

• *Don't dig more worms than you need. You'll simply deplete stocks for yourself in the future.*

• *Treat your worms carefully. Keep them in cool, moist conditions in damp newspaper. Check regularly for any worms that have died or that you have nicked with the fork without realising.*

and well into the autumn. The area also fishes well for dab, flounder and codling. Try to fish this area after a good easterly blow, especially if you can fish into darkness on the flood. The Sea Palling and Waxham reefs offer really exciting new possibilities. They are part of a fifteen-mile scheme designed to protect those beaches of the Norfolk coast that are particularly susceptible to erosion. Something like 100,000 tonnes of sand and shingle are lost to the tides each year. Eight reefs have been constructed so far to steady this process. Four of the reefs are enormous – 250 yards in length and built on thick rock mattresses. These areas were always top bass marks, and the reefs have only added to the attraction.

The presence of the reefs has caused massive build-ups of sand, and this has created horseshoe-type bays of great width. Food tends to get deposited in these areas and this attracts great numbers of whiting, flatfish, dogfish, ray and, especially, bass. When the bass move in – as they do from May onwards – they are feeding hard and bites are frenzied. You can bait-fish on the lead or even use a float. Plugging has become increasingly popular amongst local anglers. All the reefs are producing fish, but the north reef to the left of Sea Palling is considered the top mark by many locals.

⊨ ACCOMMODATION – phone the Tourist Information Centre in Great Yarmouth on 01493 842195 for advice on accommodation in the area.

○ TACKLE SHOPS – see the entries for Great Yarmouth (below).

GREAT YARMOUTH

Great Yarmouth itself is a real hubbub of a place and not to everyone's taste. Nevertheless, however you view the bustling tourist trade in the town, you can't deny that Great Yarmouth has all styles of sea fishing on offer – two piers, miles of perfect shoreline and two mouths of well-wharved river from the harbour's mouth to the Haven bridge. You will also find plenty of boat angling.

There are lots of good marks around the Yarmouth area. The Pyramid, for example, gives up codling and bass. The Big Dipper and Green Shelter produce cod, with good numbers coming from the jetty. Altogether a pulsating area!

I've personally done well in the harbour at Gorleston on Sea for mullet during the summer. I haven't picked up any big fish, but the mullet swarm there in great numbers during the right conditions. And for a really special treat, you can't beat going out for a day afloat.

📖 ACCOMMODATION – information about accommodation in the area can be obtained from the Tourist Information Centre in Great Yarmouth on 01493 842195.

⭕ TACKLE SHOPS – the tackle shops hereabouts offer really good advice – try Dave Docwra on 01493 843563. Gorleston Tackle Centre on 01493 662448 also gives up-to-the-minute advice. Tackle 'n' Tide on 01493 852221 has a good reputation.

🛥 BOAT HIRE – contact Bishop Boat Services on 01493 664739.

LOWESTOFT

Continuing south, Lowestoft is the next major centre, and it's noted for cod through the autumn, winter and spring, along with whiting and flatfish, and tope and ray from the charter boats.

Lowestoft harbour is a centre for really good flounder fishing, especially on crabs, with some codling and bass probable. There are good beaches to be found both north and south of the town, and the North Beach is a favourite mark.

📖 ACCOMMODATION – the Tourist Information Centre in Lowestoft can advise on accommodation in the area; phone them on 01502 533600.

⭕ TACKLE SHOPS – Ted Bean Fishing Tackle on 01502 565832 and Sam Hook Sports on 01502 565821 are both excellent tackle shops offering good practical advice.

SOUTHWOLD

The Kessingland area has quite a bit to offer, but the fishing really comes alive again at Southwold. This is a lovely town, justifiably popular with anglers and tourists alike, so if you fancy a bit of a holiday with some excellent sea fishing thrown in, then you just can't beat heading down the A12 to Southwold.

Lying just twelve miles south of Lowestoft and forty-five miles north of Ipswich, Southwold is a delightful coastal town, small and quiet, but offering a great deal – good accommodation, great pubs, nice shopping and lovely scenery. The harbour to the south of the town is small, but bustling. You can fish along the harbour wall, and you will find some good flounders available in the spring and bass throughout the summer. Try spinning or float fishing, along with light legering. The pier was in a sorry state, but it's now being rebuilt, and this will add a lot to the shore potential of the town. Bass are almost certain to figure in captures.

There are beaches everywhere in Southwold and they produce a few sole in the summer. Bass, too, show up. In the winter, the favourites are cod and whiting. You'll find the sea wall as you head southwards, towards

Go on, treat yourself. This really is one of the most highly recommended day's bass fishing you could possibly hope to have. Go out with Stewart Smalley, the Aldeburgh tackle dealer, who runs his twenty-foot boat out of Orford from May through to October.

This may seem a small boat, but it's supremely safe, very well skippered and highly manoeuvrable. Also, being a light craft, you do feel as though the fishing is very close and intimate. Stewart is extremely safety conscious and only takes very small groups, so don't worry. Enjoy!

This part of the Suffolk coastline is an absolute gem, and Orford itself is the prettiest village imaginable. Stewart generally, however, takes you from the quay, down the Ore estuary. You'll see birds and even the odd seal. He'll be heading for sandbanks about eighteen miles offshore where the bass really fight well on light gear. You'll be fishing on the drift, often with live sand eels. It's quick, lively, entertaining fishing, and if the bass are feeding you can expect quite a haul. Many of them aren't huge fish, but you can bank on five-pounders at the very least. And don't they scrap on light gear in that quick flowing water? It's a good idea, Stewart says, to use braid as main line. This keeps you in the closest of contact with what's going on and you will feel bites instantly. The thrill of the battle is also enhanced on non-stretch line.

During the day, there's also the chance to have a crack for the odd turbot or brill – in fact, Stewart says he's taking parties out now specifically for these. At around £200 to hire the boat, it's not the cheapest day out you'll ever have, but you won't regret a single penny of the cost. Stewart is a great character, with a huge knowledge of this part of the world and how the bass act in it. A day to remember. You can contact Stewart at Aldeburgh Tackle on 01728 454030.

To get the best out of your day with Stewart – or any day after bass, come to that – make sure you have the necessary gear. If you fancy lure fishing, which is truly sporting and great fun, you'll need a variety of spoons, spinners, plugs, pirks and jelly lures. Phone Cornish Lures on 01872 223346 and try their Scandinavian-type mini pirks. Eddystone (on 01752 696161) make the fabulous Eddyjelly sandeel lures that are almost better than the real thing. The Harris Angling Company (on 01692 581208) still offer the widest range of lures for the bass angler, and their brilliant catalogue is a must. Finally, if you want to go the full mile and try fly fishing for bass, contact Danny at Sportfish on 01544 327111.

PIER-FISHING TIPS

Preparation

• If the pier dries out at low water, it pays to walk around looking for fish-holding features. Check out gullies, rough ground and mussel beds.

• Familiarise yourself with pier rules and restrictions. Some only allow underarm casting or one rod per angler. Check closing times and charges.

• Ask a local tackle dealer to point you in the right direction as to the best parts of the pier and the best stages of the tide to fish them. Check out the weather – high waves can sometimes crash over exposed areas.

Equipment

• You'll always need a drop net because you just never know when that monster might come along.

• If you're after mullet or garfish, take ground bait and a suitable bag.

• A length of thin rope is always useful for lowering a bucket down to the water if you need to keep bait or fish fresh during the day.

• As you can't rely on seating, it's a good idea if your tackle box can double up as a chair.

Methods

• If you need to cast long, use a longer leader than you would consider for beach fishing. When you're swinging a decent fish up towards you, you want the security of knowing that the leader knot is on the reel and not halfway down the pier stanchions .

• Fish next to the girders for pollack, wrasse and pouting.

• During the summer, try float fishing on freshwater gear for pollack, mackerel, garfish and bass.

• Experiment with baits – a live prawn, for example, can work wonders. Also, twitch baits back and keep them on the move – guaranteed to attract the attention of a flatfish.

The Net Result

• If you've got a good fish on, try to get help from a nearby angler. He can lower the net down into the water, downtide of the fish, so that you can bring the fish to the net and not vice versa.

• If a big fish goes with the tide under the pier, try to get a fellow angler to net it as it comes out the other side. Don't drag it back against a heavy tide or you're almost bound to lose it.

the pier, and this fishes well throughout the year. Here you'll get bass, again, from May right through into the autumn, along with sole. If you want to go out, charter boats run from the town. You can expect some great sport from tope, pollack and cod. You'll also pick up some very nice bass indeed.

Just to the south of the town lies Blythe Water, an expanse of water that opens to the sea and forms a safe mooring area for commercial working boats. These are available to take you out over the numerous wrecks off the East Anglian coast. Many of the wrecks are old World War II hulks. Summer wrecking, in particular, can be excellent. Summer perking, therefore, is a real possibility – the local skippers have the latest gear and know exactly where to go. Cod to twenty pounds are more than possible.

It's also worth having a look at the mouth of the River Blythe itself if you fancy doing a little bit of exploring. Access isn't always easy and do take great care of the sometimes treacherous marshes hereabouts. Don't take any risks with the tide, as it can come in very quickly. You'll find eels and flatfish in the area and, from June onwards, increasing numbers of mullet.

The coastline all the way from Southwold down to Dunwich throws up some very good whiting during the winter months, albeit fish that move in small shoals. Dunwich is also a very popular flounder venue. Don't discount the Minsmere area, either, for the odd good cod and flounder once the colder weather moves in.

All in all, this is a very interesting piece of coastline with Southwold at its core. It is an area of outstanding natural beauty, and if you're one of those sea anglers who takes an interest in bird life, then you're in for a magnificent treat.

⊨ **ACCOMMODATION** – call the Lowestoft Tourist Information Centre on 01502 533600.
○ **TACKLE SHOPS** – the local tackle shop, Southwold Angling Centre, is a mine of information; phone them on 01502 722085.
⛵ **BOAT HIRE** – contact Nigel Hayter on 017885 316429 or Dave Wright on 01502 722411.

ALDEBURGH, FELIXSTOWE AND HARWICH

Travelling south, the town of Aldeburgh is well worth a look. This beautiful old town offers really consistent sport with codling and gives up some good bass. Also look for mullet in the summer months. You'll find these fascinating fish all the way down the coast past Orford and along the River Ore. The River Deben, too, is home to swarms of these fish during the summer months. They're not easy to catch, but the sport can be tremendous if you pick the right method at the right height of the water.

21

Felixstowe and Harwich both offer marvellous opportunities. Bass well into double figures have come from the sea front at Felixstowe and from marks close to Harwich harbour and Dovercourt. Codling tend to dominate Suffolk's beach catches here, but from the boats that can be chartered locally you'll pick up plenty of stingray and thornback.

A word here about the pier at Felixstowe, which has become a really popular sea-angling venue throughout the year. It's easy to fish and easy to find, just down the A14 from Ipswich. It doesn't matter what the conditions, you'll find the fish. It's a great place for garfish, and you'll pick up sole after dark during the summer months. There's always the chance of a specimen bass as well. After dark is the best time, once everything becomes a little bit quieter, but do check closing times so you're not locked on! Generally, it closes around 10:00pm. If you're fishing during the daylight, try to pick a day when there's a bit of a chop and not too much sunshine. The best baits are lugworm, squid and mackerel, although the soles go well on ragworm, and peeler crabs can't be beaten for big bass. The pier also allows for fishing during rough weather when you'd be forced off the beach.

This area is particularly renowned for boat fishing, especially in the winter, when the weather can be somewhat inclement. The rivers Orwell and Stour meet here, separating Harwich and Felixstowe with an expanse of water about a mile wide. This produces a natural harbour. Harwich still maintains its olde-worlde, dignified charm, whereas Felixstowe has become something of a candyfloss paradise. Also, Felixstowe harbour is becoming one of the most advanced in the world, as it is dredged to accommodate enormous container vessels. Given the prevailing westerly winds, this area offers tremendous boat-fishing possibilities, especially through the winter. Winter fishing can take place less than a mile offshore on well-known marks such as the Outer Ridge, and Felixstowe or Wadgate ledges. Expect whiting from September, and codling to move in the following month. There are also good bass hanging around throughout the autumn period.

Every year, towards the end of November, the Shotley Cod Competition is held slap-bang in the middle of this productive area. No matter how rough the conditions may be, boats go out and fish are caught. You can expect to find codling of between three and six pounds, and double-figure fish do show up as well. As yet, there are no official charter boats working the area, but it's possible to launch your own craft at either the Suffolk Yacht Harbour or the Shotley Marina, which is well-designed and offers every possible facility, or you might hire a boat.

BOAT SAFETY

If you fancy getting afloat, remember that safety is absolutely paramount. Plan every trip in a professional sort of way, take a real personal pride in your boat and ensure that it's in tiptop condition.

• *If your engine dies, drop anchor and stabilise the situation. Make sure that you have sufficient anchor chain and rope to hold bottom.*

• *Keep calm. A breakdown is a mind-numbing experience but gather your composure as quickly as possible and start asking for help.*

• *Don't rely on a mobile phone for talking to lifeboats or rescue helicopters. You need a properly installed VHF to get you through to the emergency services or neighbouring boats.*

• *Don't be afraid to admit that you've got a problem. As soon as you sense danger, make that call. Act swiftly and don't let a crisis develop.*

• *Make sure you carry spares and know how to use them. Familiarise yourself with your boat and its engine.*

• *Listen to the regular weather bulletins put out by your local coastguard every few hours. If there's a sudden change in the weather, head for shore.*

• *There's always a chance you might have to wait for help, so always take life-jackets, warm clothing, food, water and flasks with you.*

• *Make sure that you have flares on board with you, particularly at night.*

• *Always tell somebody where you are going. If you change your plans, phone through the information.*

• *No matter how good the fishing is, don't leave it too late to return to port as this can be very worrying for those on shore.*

• *Always try to give the coastguard your exact position.*

• *Make sure you and everyone on your boat is wearing a life-jacket.*

• *Drinking alcohol is unacceptable out at sea – especially if you're the skipper. Keep a clear head at all times and make sure anybody fishing with you does the same.*

• *It's a good idea to have alternative means of propulsion. Stick an old engine, for example, somewhere down in the boat's hold. Even a pair of oars can make a difference.*

• *Charts are useful, and always have a compass with you.*

• *If you're a novice boat owner, join your local club for some expert advice and tuition.*

• *If you're fishing with a group of friends, for example, make sure they all know the ins and outs of your boat and what they would have to do in an emergency.*

⊨ **ACCOMMODATION** – contact the Tourist Information Offices in Aldeburgh on 01728 453637, Felixstowe on 01394 276770 or Harwich on 01255 506139.

○ **TACKLE SHOPS** – visit Aldeburgh Tackle at 30 Crabbe Street, or phone 01728 454030.

⊯ **BOAT HIRE** – for boats, contact Barton's Marina on 01255 503552 or Vick Caunter on 01255 552855 in Harwich.

WALTON ON THE NAZE AND CLACTON-ON-SEA

Walton on the Naze is another major sea-fishing centre offering cod, skate, mullet and dab. Concentrate on the pier and, slightly further south, on Frinton Wall and Frinton sea front.

There's more good summer fishing down at Clacton-on-Sea from the beach, the pier and the many commercial boats. You'll find dabs, plaice, bass, eels, thornbacks, tope and dogfish.

⊨ **ACCOMMODATION** – contact Clacton-on-Sea Tourist Information Centre on 01255 423400.

○ **TACKLE SHOPS** – quite the best tackle shop in the area is John Metcalfe's, to be found at 15 Newgate Street, Walton on the Naze on 01255 675680. You can also contact Brian Dean's Tackle Shop on 01255 425992 for details on baits and permits and for general information.

⊯ **BOAT HIRE** – contact Mr S. Murphy on 01255 674274.

THE RIVER CROUCH

The River Crouch is a fascinating and little-known river that joins the Thames estuary. It's sandwiched between the Thames and the Blackwater. If you're a shore angler, you'll find mullet, bass, flounder and eels through the summer. There's a well-known area called the Hole, which you'll find half a mile or so from the Essex Marina, based at Wallasea. You can fish here along an accessible stretch of sea wall. Night is generally the best time, especially in the summer when the water is warm, and you might be lucky enough to see the mullet finning or the bass actually hunting. There is also some bank space at Burnham-on-Crouch. Peeler crabs are a preferred bait for the bass, while rag and lug are good for flounder and eel. Also, expect to pick up whiting on the worm. Obviously, you can use normal beach casting gear here but I really recommend light spinning tackle for the bass if you're going to get the best out of your sport.

The boat angler is also well catered for on the Crouch. Essex Marina is the centre for all boat traffic here, and it has just undergone a major refurbishment. There's a brand new boat hoist, new boat shed and electric

Lugworms are a terrific bait – especially for winter cod. A professional digger would hope for anything between 700 and 1,000 worms in a session.

As the sun begins to set, many fish come closer inshore and a very long cast is not always necessary. This is especially applicable after a strong wind.

Typical mullet territory – throughout the summer months, these nomads of the sea like to investigate estuaries, creeks and backwaters, where they find abundant food.

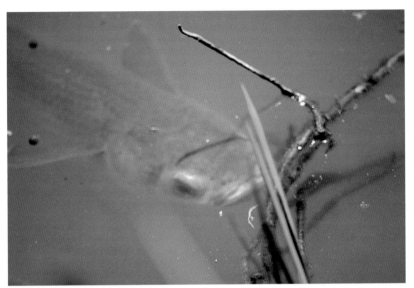

A fascinating close-up of a mullet feeding. This fish is simply browsing on the surface vegetation looking for minute food particles.

Rock fishing in the Channel Islands. Find some rocks and you've really stumbled onto a fish-holding feature. Expect conger, wrasse and bass during the summer months.

The harbours of Devon and Cornwall hold eels, dab and even intrepid bass. They're good places for beginners to learn and for adults, too, if the sea outside is particularly rough.

This Jumping Jack is typical of the new breed of artificial lures now available. It often pays to think of using a plastic lure rather than real fish, worms or crabs.

and water points around the hard-standing areas. A new bar and restaurant complex has been planned and is probably already in operation. You'll find toilets, showers and free parking. There's a slipway and constant water, so it's a perfect place for anglers who wish to bring their own boats. There is a charge, though, for using the facility.

It's very easy to charter a boat in this area. The Crouch is a small river and is sheltered, so the boats hardly ever have to cancel a trip. There are plenty of fish available, too, and this is pretty much a year-round venue. In the spring, you'll find good thornbacks only twenty minutes or so from the marina, along with codling, smooth-hound and bass. Indeed, the Thames estuary has been famous for years for all these species, including tope and even angler fish.

Up-tiding is the most common method, although down-tiding is also used. The water tends to be quite murky, so artificial lures are rarely tried. Favourite baits are worms, squid and peeler crabs. The nearest tackle shops are to be found at Southend-on-Sea, but the skippers all supply bait and tackle so you won't run short.

ACCOMMODATION – the Tourist Information Centre in Southend-on-Sea on 01702 215120 can advise on accommodation available in the area.

TACKLE SHOPS – see below for tackle shops in Southend-on-Sea.

BOAT HIRE – highly recommended skippers include Dave Godwin on 01702 308043, Andy Hide on 01268 451891, Andy Lambert on 01702 218932 and Steve Smith on 07831 363629.

SOUTHEND-ON-SEA

Southend-on-Sea is another town offering fantastic pier fishing, especially for flounders and school bass. Mullet are common in the summer, along with mackerel, scad and garfish. Plaice are also a target species, with cod, codling and large flounders in the winter. The pier also fishes well for whiting until late December. A small charge is levied for day permits.

ACCOMMODATION – the Tourist Information Centre in Southend-on-Sea on 01702 215120 can advise on accommodation available in the area.

TACKLE SHOPS – try either Jetty Anglers in Southend-on-Sea on 01702 611826 or the Southend Angling Centre on 01702 603303 for up-to-the-minute advice.

BOAT HIRE – Southend has a thriving charter-boat fleet. Try the *Skerry Belle* on 01702 390842, Dave Godwin's *Creditor* on 01702 308043, the *Dawn Breaker* on 01702 469114 or the *Nitricia* on 01268 272179.

SEA-FISHING SITES IN SOUTH-EAST ENGLAND

Foreshore

Sand bank

N

ESSEX

Harwich

Braintree

Colchester

The Naze

A120

Witham

Brightlingsea

M11

Clacton-on-Sea

Harlow

Chelmsford

Enfield

Chigwell

Brentwood

M25

A406

A12

M1

A10

A13

A127

LONDON

Woolwich

Foulness Island

M25

Southend-on-Sea

A40

Richmond

Dartford Bridge

R.Thames

M

A20

Dartford

Gravesend

Sheerness

Herne Bay

Margate

Staines

Croydon

Swanley

Rochester

Isle of Sheppey

Isle of Thanet

Kingsgate

Botany Bay

Ramsgate

Dumpton Gap

Chatham

Faversham

River Stour

Pegwell Bay

Woking

M25

M25

M20

A2

Canterbury

Sandwich Bay

Guildford

Dorking

Sevenoaks

Maidstone

M20

North

M2

Deal

Farnham

A31

M23

A21

East Grinstead

Tunbridge Wells

Ashford

Downs

A28

SURREY

A26

KENT

Dover

Haslemere

Crawley

Romney Marsh

Sandgate

Folkestone

30m

Hythe

Dymchurch

Strait of Dover

Midhurst

Haywards Heath

River Ouse

Uckfield

A264

Rye

50m

A24

A23

Hurstpierpoint

A26

EAST SUSSEX

A259

Rye Bay

WEST SUSSEX

River Adur

River Cuckmere

Hailsham

A271

Dungeness

Chichester

Worthing

South Downs

Lewes

Alfriston

Hastings

A27

Brighton

(Marina and Pier)

Newhaven

St Leonards

Bognor Regis

Littlehampton

Piddinghoe

Seaford

Pevensey Bay

Langney Point

Sovereign Harbour

Selsey Bill

Eastbourne

Beachy Head

E N G L I S H   C H A N N E L

30m

50m

❝ *I've fished pretty well all my life out of Pevensey Bay and I've never once become dissatisfied or wished for something more dramatic. The area, as far as I can see, has got everything for the sea angler. There's some terrific beach fishing around. There are piers, if that's what you fancy, as well as marinas, rocky headlands and some tremendous boat fishing. The bass fishing in the summer is hard to beat, and I've seen some great winter codding through the course of my fishing career. This is also a really good area for the dinghy enthusiast, but launch sites are limited along the coast. Having your own craft really does make you that little bit more independent and, especially during the warmer months, can get you out to the best marks where there's little competition for places. This is also a great area for the match man, with comprehensive lists of shore and boat matches throughout the year. There are great tackle shops, lots of holiday resorts and it's all very scenic. In short, it's as good for the holidaying angler as it is for the resident.* ❞

JIM WHIPPY, EDITOR OF *BOAT FISHING* MAGAZINE

I'd like to emphasise the point that Jim makes about the holiday potential for the angler along this area of coastline. Some of the resorts that we're looking at here – Brighton and Eastbourne, for example – really do offer the entire holiday package. I caught my first mullet down here many years ago when I was a student in London. I got totally fed up with the park ponds in the capital and decided to head south to the coast. The gear that I had been using for small carp and tench proved absolutely ideal for the mullet – and believe me, they fought twice as hard! And, being a student, I was quite pleased to have something to take back for the kitchen. Not that I would do that now, even though mullet numbers aren't really threatened. For me, the biggest thrill of all is to see a fish swim away wild and free.

SHEERNESS

Situated on the north coast of the Isle of Sheppey, Sheerness is a famous area for cod and whiting from the autumn onwards. This has been the long-time venue of the British Open, which is held towards the end of the year when the cod have, hopefully, arrived.

Some of the famous marks include Barton's Point, East Church Gap and New Sea Wall. The Isle of Sheppey is easily reached from the M2 by turning off north at junction 5.

⊨ ACCOMMODATION – phone the Tourist Information Centre in Sheerness on 01795 668061.

○ TACKLE SHOPS – Island Bait and Tackle Shop on 01795 668506 is the hub of the area, selling fresh bait and dispensing up-to-the-minute information.

HERNE BAY

Moving east, we come to the charming Kentish town of Herne Bay, which offers the sea angler some really good spring fishing. You can expect flounders and some of the earliest bass around the British shores. Peeler crab is one of the favourite baits, and can be bought locally. As the season progresses, the bass become more common and move up into the shallow warm water where they can be caught very close to the beach. Lugworm begins to come into its own, but spinning is even more exciting. If the sea looks reasonably clear, try anything that catches the light. Silver and gold spoons are particularly effective. However, if the water is calm, you can even catch bass in shallow water on surface-working lures – brilliantly exciting.

Remember that long casting isn't always essential and you will quite often find bass working very close inshore looking for food. When the bass are in close, you will soon discover that stealth is much more important than brawn. In fact, when you're bass fishing near to the beach like this, it's important to take a leaf out of our freshwater-fishing cousins' book and avoid crunching on the shingle.

As the summer progresses, the bass remain plentiful, but you will also find plenty of black bream, dogfish and even some stingray that can be caught from the beaches. As the autumn progresses, you can expect an influx of whiting.

⊨ ACCOMMODATION – phone the Tourist Information Centre in Herne Bay on 01227 361911.

○ TACKLE SHOPS – Herne Bay Angling on 01227 362127 or Ron Edwards Tackle on 01227 372517.

MARGATE

This well-known holiday centre features some tremendous fishing. One of Margate's great advantages is the wide variety of fishing on offer. It's suitable for all levels of angling ability – from the expert angler down to the novice who just wants a few hours with the children in the middle of a summer Bank Holiday. Margate is particularly noted for its very good bass fishing, which you can do either from the shore or, preferably, from a boat using spinning gear. Keep on the move until you find the fish, and also scan the waters for any surface disturbance through binoculars. Expect to see small fish breaking the surface, or a cluster of gulls gathering as bass force prey fish upwards.

Come the winter, Margate's pier is excellent for cod and whiting – certainly from November through to April or May. There's also some excellent rock fishing at nearby Botany Bay, Dumpton Gap and Kingsgate. You'll also find that there are opportunities to do a little bit of tope fishing by boat. The shallow, warm water off Margate is perfect for these hard-fighting species. Don't over-gun yourself or you won't get the best out of your fishing. In fact, heavy carp gear is just about right. Don't go too low on line strength, however – the last thing you want to do is leave fish with hooks in them.

⊨ ACCOMMODATION – phone the Tourist Information Centre in Margate on 01843 230203.
○ TACKLE SHOPS – contact Kingfisheries on 01843 223866.

RAMSGATE

Another top traditional holidaying area in the south east, Ramsgate can – like its neighbour Margate – become very busy in the summer, when the beaches are probably best fished early or late. However, Ramsgate offers both harbour and pier fishing and the area comes very much into its own when the tourists leave and the cod arrive!

Once again, expect some really good bass fishing, along with excellent flatfish and some thornbacks. Ramsgate's attractive little harbour is home to a vibrant little fishing fleet so, providing the weather is clement, you will be able to get offshore most days of the year. Goodwin Sands is one of the traditional hotspots, producing tope, flatfish, skate and bass.

⊨ ACCOMMODATION – Ramsgate has a wide range of accommodation and the Tourist Information Centre on 01843 583333/4 will be able to supply you with details.
○ TACKLE SHOPS – contact Fisherman's Corner Tackle Shop on 01843 582174.
⊷ BOAT HIRE – contact Mr Spencer, skipper of *Any Chance*, on 01843 835353.

THE STOUR ESTUARY

Sandwich Bay and the River Stour offer some very interesting fishing indeed. Entrance to the bay is by a private toll road that takes you to a wonderful, unspoilt area. There's some very good beach fishing, but one of the main delights, come the summer, is the grey mullet that run up the river. Mind you, these mullet can be fiendishly difficult to catch and they are totally unpredictable.

Mullet fishing is an art all to itself. Sometimes you'll find that they're truly switched on and you can catch them on almost any bait going. Most of the time, however, they'll have you absolutely tearing your hair out in frustration and wondering where on earth you're going wrong. Hook one, however, and the fun really begins. In fact, pound for pound, they're probably the hardest fighting fish in saltwater – on reasonably light gear, that is.

⊨ ACCOMMODATION – phone the Tourist Information Centre in Sandwich on 01304 613565.

○ TACKLE SHOPS – for all your bait and tackle needs, try the Sandwich Bait and Tackle shop on 01304 613752.

DEAL AND DOVER

You'll find some very interesting possibilities around Deal – Admiralty Pier is a good mark and available for a small daily fee – but Dover is, perhaps, the main attraction of this particular area, offering excellent boat and beach fishing. Some tremendous cod are taken from nearby wrecks, and there's excellent shore fishing from Shakespeare Beach. The Prince of Wales Pier is also a magnet and a perfect place for novices, offering the possibility of big mixed bags.

⊨ ACCOMMODATION – phone the Tourist Information Centre in Deal on 01304 369576 or that in Dover on 01304 205108.

○ TACKLE SHOPS – Channel Angling on 01304 373104 will provide bait, tackle and information On the Deal area. In Dover, phone Bill's Bait and Tackle on 01304 201457.

FOLKESTONE

Folkestone is often overshadowed by Dover, its big neighbour, but this shouldn't be the case because it really has got the lot – boat, beach and pier fishing. It is also more and more in the public eye as the gateway to Europe, standing as it does at the English end of the Channel Tunnel.

The Warren, which leads away under the cliffs on the east side of Folkestone, has some good summer fishing from May and June onwards, with bass coming on the early tides, and soles and pouting appearing near the top as darkness approaches. You'll start to find whiting and codling as winter moves in. Access to the fishing can be tricky and the best spots, as always, involve a good walk.

Next we come to Folkestone Sands, which run from Copt Point to the pier. The bottom is snag free, so it's easy fishing and it offers up small flatfish and school bass. Rotunda Beach shelves steeply and runs from the west side of the pier. Depth means that long casting isn't essential, and bass, cod and flatfish can be caught close in.

Lower Sandgate Road, which runs from Metropol Rocks to Mermaid Point, is very rocky and offers some good summer fishing from its two big concrete groynes.

The pier runs a good 400 yards out from Rotunda Beach and is accessible for a small fee. Tickets can be bought from the local tackle shops. Most locals make for the end section of the pier where there are fewer snags and where it fishes well over low water. The pier has a history of some big fish and offers a very comfortable fishing platform. It's also a good spot for conger and has produced fish over forty pounds in weight. The locals are convinced, however, that there are much bigger conger in the huge snags at the base of the pier wall. July to October seems to be the best time – try fresh mackerel as bait.

Bass fishing is an important feature of the Folkestone scene. These fish drift around all year long, although the traditional season is May until autumn. Float fishing and light spinning make headway in the shoals of school bass, and you'll also pick up garfish. Generally, the bigger bass come later on in the year, and as autumn approaches you can expect these larger fish to come in close, especially at night. Early bass seem to prefer peeler crab and ragworm, but later in the year, small live baits will do the trick. Also, try spinning with large spoons whenever the sea is reasonably clear.

There's a lively boat-fishing scene, most of which is done over the famous Varne Bank or the Ridge and the French Holes. Expect to pick up turbot, plaice and thornbacks. Pirking for cod is also a favourite. There are also some productive wrecks and the inshore cod fishing is excellent in the winter.

ACCOMMODATION – Folkestone Tourist Information Centre on 01303 358594 will give you all the advice you need on accommodation.

TACKLE SHOPS – Folkestone Angling on 01303 253881 or Harbour Tackle on 01303 220763 will advise on skippers, bait, conditions and general fishing hotspots.

BOAT HIRE – boats include the *Enterprise* on 01303 252513, *Folkestone Angler* on 01303 893264, *Pathfinder* on 01322 669159 and *Virginia Warrior* on 01622 207134.

And how about old Father Thames himself – the river of comebacks? You're even getting cod there again these days, right up as far as Dartford Bridge. This is very muddy water, so you don't have to worry too much about having to fish at night. Most of the fish are comparatively small, but some are very decent indeed, with the odd double-figure specimen.

Shorn Mede lighthouse at Gravesend is a particular hotspot. It's not the easiest place to get to and it is a good long walk – some of it over thick mud. You do need to get out so that you can fish in the drop-off on the edge of the shipping lanes. The tide run here can be quite fierce, but four or five ounces of weight should do, providing you cast uptide and let a belly of line develop. Bites are generally straightforward slack liners. You don't want too strong a tide – around six yards is about right. Add to that a wind from the south or south west and you're really in – a strong wind will help you cast out even further. Lugworm seems to be a great bait, whilst a lug and squid combination tends to attract whiting.

If fishing the bank isn't quite what you're after, think about going afloat. Lee Bollingbroke on 01255 432871 is running a charter boat out of Brightlingsea, the port on the north side of the Thames estuary. His parties take good bags of cod throughout the winter and there's some tremendous bass and smooth-hound fishing through the summer; expect some thornbacks as well. A great day out.

There are plenty of good tackle shops in the area that can give advice – try Strood Angling on 01634 721300, Maidstone Angling on 01622 677326, Medway Tackle on 01634 570740 and the Dartford Angling Centre on 01322 228532.

THE ROMNEY COAST

Sandgate, Hythe and Dungeness all offer some good fishing possibilities from both beach and boats. Expect bass, codling, whiting and conger. Hythe is also well-known for its army ranges. You can't fish here all the time because it's still actively used by the army and there's a list of firing times on display at either end of the range. When the army is actually present and carrying out operations, access is guarded by sentries. The range is on the A259 between Hythe and Dymchurch and you'll find some parking spaces on the verge of the road. One of the best times to approach the range is over Christmas when there's a week or so without any activity and it's safe to fish. Happily, this coincides with the arrival of some very good cod in decent numbers. For a number of years, there has been an annual match held during this period. The fact that the number of anglers just seems to keep going up must be a testament to the standard of the fishing. You can't take your car past the access point, so you're faced with a long walk to get to some of the best marks – travel light. You'll find that the range is basically a mix of shingle and sand, with groynes at intervals.

Locals favour the mark known as the Broken Tower, an old Martello tower that has been a gunnery target for a long time. You'll find this about a mile from the Dymchurch end of the range. It's also good as there is deep water close to a sandbar and you don't have to cast too far out.

The range fishes particularly well after a good wind, at rising and high water and up to a couple of hours down. Night is also a time favoured by the locals. Then you will pick up cod, codling, flatfish and some whiting in the winter months. Earlier in the year, you will also find bass about. All the usual baits are used with success here, including lug and squid. Cocktails are also a proven favourite.

Before leaving this area, let's have a look at Dymchurch promenade, which you will find joining on virtually from the southern end of the Hythe range. This is a sea wall that runs along the Dymchurch road. There are two particular areas favoured by the locals, especially in the winter when it's considered one of the top marks of the area. About midway along the promenade, you will come to Willop sluice. This is a culvert that channels out water overflowing from Romney Marsh that needs to get into the sea. The other place the locals favour is called the Redoubt, which you will find right at the end of the Hythe range itself. Here, once again, there's deep water close in and long casting isn't considered necessary.

The fishing is generally quite easy, but you should watch out for the remains of old groynes, which can prove to be major snags, especially if there is a heavy wind or strong tidal currents. In these conditions, you should also beware of the concrete wall itself, because the foothold can be precarious when it's drenched.

Most of the locals think the area is best attacked from half-tide up to half-tide down. However, in rough weather – which means a south-westerly wind – even low tide can be worth trying. This is obviously a very convenient spot for summer bass and flatfish but it fishes particularly well after dark, around high water for codling and, especially, whiting, which are numerous. For bass, a top tip is to get out very early in the morning, especially when the sea is calm, and watch carefully for fish hunting close in. A pair of binoculars can be a useful aid. Peeler crab can be good, but why not try light spinning gear for maximum mobility and sport? Use an eight- to nine-foot rod, fixed spool reel loaded with eight-pound line for maximum casting range, and take an assortment of silver spoons and spinners.

As a last thought, do take care where you park, and keep away from the various access roads and holiday camp entrances.

⊨ Accommodation – for details of accommodation in the area, phone the Tourist Information Centre in Hythe on 01303 267799.

○ Tackle shops – contact Romney Tackle on 01797 363990, Marsh Tackle in Dymchurch on 01303 873020 or try Mick Sullivan of Mick's Tackle Shop in Hythe. Mick is also involved in the organisation of any matches held in this area; he can be contacted on 01303 266334.

RYE, HASTINGS AND ST LEONARDS

Rye harbour is another place where you can expect mullet during the summer months. Moving west, Hastings offers some top sea fishing from its pier and boats – it's a centre for tope, bass, conger, flatfish and codling and whiting, especially later in the year. Hastings also hosts an international sea-angling festival in October.

New Church at St Leonards is just down the A259 from Hastings. The name New Church is actually the local nickname for St Leonards' Church itself, the building right on the sea front.

This is a very productive beach mark that has the additional advantage of good car parking! There's a car-park opposite the church itself. Moreover, the beach here is shingle and sand between groynes – an easy place to fish for all levels of ability. Locals consider the best time to fish to be early on the ebb tide, though the beginning of the flood can also be productive.

New Church comes into its own during the autumn and the winter. Expect good bags of codling, whiting and flatfish. Spring and summer, however, also offer tremendous possibilities for the visiting angler.

At times, there are some very good bass about, and once again the tip is to get out early and late and see what is feeding. Mobility is often the key. Also, in the summer, expect mackerel and plenty of eels, along with the occasional smooth-hound.

All the usual baits work here, but if you can't get anything more exotic than lugworm, don't worry, as this is arguably the favourite.

⊨ Accommodation – there is plenty of accommodation in the area, from hotels to bed-and-breakfasts. The Tourist Information Centre in Rye on 01797 226696, or that in Hastings on 01424 781111, can advise.

○ Tackle shops – try the Hastings Angling Centre on 01424 432178, Steve's Tackle Shop on 01424 433404 and Amber Dolphin on 01424 427005 – all in Hastings.

PEVENSEY BAY

Pevensey Bay is one of the main attractions along this part of the south coast, and there's a great deal of match angling going on due to its relatively sheltered position and consistent sport. Pevensey Bay itself is a pleasant village, not far from Eastbourne, so another good bet for the holidaying angler. What's more, the beach produces fish year round with few dull periods. The beach is some two miles in length overall, a mix of shingle and sand, with groynes at regular intervals. There are also Martello towers scattered along the shoreline.

So what do you get at Pevensey? Winter throws up great numbers of whiting, along with some codling and flatfish. Spring is productive, though mostly for small fish in great numbers, whilst the summer species include smooth-hound, dogfish, bass and plaice. There are garfish and mackerel about, but these are generally further offshore. Come autumn, the codling will move in. There will also be sole until the late autumn.

Hotspots? Well, the whole beach at Pevensey produces good numbers of fish, so virtually everywhere is worth trying. However, the Pevensey Bay Aqua Club, in the middle of the beach, is considered one of the better marks, and a lot of locals head towards the bungalows that can be found near the eastern end of the beach. Most local advice suggests that the most productive state of the tide would be the first two hours of the flood and the first two of the ebb. Go for all the usual baits, including lugworm, ragworm, squid, peeler crab and various forms of fish. Lug can be dug or pumped at low tide.

Let's just focus briefly on the bass fishing. There are some very good bass around, with fish over double figures a distinct possibility. These can come along at any time, to any method, but past history seems to suggest that a large fish bait is perhaps the best of all. Try half a mackerel or perhaps a smelt. If you hook up one of these semi-frozen, you'll find that you will be able to cast it a good long distance, especially if you tie it to the line with an elastic band. The same goes for another excellent, smelly, oily bait – sardine.

Look for some feature to cast to. For example, there are pipes running into the sea at various intervals and these often attract fish. Alternatively, keep on the move and work the bait a little bit. Be prepared for a big bite from a big fish. There are also plenty of small bass in the two- to four-pound bracket, especially throughout the summer. Lug are perfectly sufficient for fish of this size. Probably your best time is on a flood tide, very early in the morning before the holidaymakers begin to swarm in numbers. It's a really good idea to put these small bass – indeed all bass come to that – back alive. Perhaps keep one for the table but no more. That way we can all rely on sport to come.

☞ **ACCOMMODATION** – the Tourist Information Centre in Hastings on 01424 781111 can advise on accommodation.

○ **TACKLE SHOPS** – for more detailed information and all the gear you're likely to need, phone the Anglers' Den in Pevensey Bay on 01323 460441.

EASTBOURNE

Eastbourne is really one of the jewels of South-East England, and caters very much for the more discerning holidaymaker. It nestles snugly under the cliffs of Beachy Head and is a world away from the razzamatazz that you'll find in many resorts. In fact, its sheltered position has led to the nickname 'suntrap of the south'. The Sovereign Harbour draws in yachts and cruisers from both England and the Continent.

If the town itself offers a haven to the tourist, then the sea gives bounty to the angler. Shore fishing ranges from heavy ground through to shingle beaches, and this means a good variety of fish is waiting to be caught. One popular mark is White Horses, accessible from the Pevensey Bay side of Langney Point. Aim for the Bay View caravan site and you'll find parking along part of the road. It's a great spot for the summer angler because at high tide the water is deep enough for the mackerel shoals to come inshore, where they can be caught on spinners. At night, you'll find sole feeding, and during the earlier part of the year, you'll pick up plenty of dab. It's a good autumn area for whiting, bass and codling.

Langney Point itself is also a good mark, and links up with the west arm of Sovereign Harbour. Here, you'll find massive boulders that were brought in from Norway to provide a good, firm shelter. You'll find garfish and mackerel in the summer, along with sole, dab and bass. There's a good run of whiting and codling in the winter.

Splash Point is a very central, convenient mark, very close to the World War II tank on the sea front. It's part of the promenade and gives much better access than the beach, so it's a handy place to fish.

Between Splash Point and the pier is a favourite local mark called Cambridge Road. There are good catches of flatfish and whiting, with quality cod and bass showing up occasionally; try lugworm and white rag. At low tide, you'll see the lugworm diggers in action.

The pier is particularly vibrant and offers very good general fishing for bass, pollack, flatfish, pouting and garfish. There are also some good mackerel to be caught throughout the summer. It's a fine spot for cod and whiting in the winter.

If it's bass that you fancy, try the Wish Tower. It's not a heavily fished mark, and perhaps that's its secret. However, cast a crab or a lugworm

FISHING FOR MULLET

Mullet are one of our most interesting species. They are often called the grey ghosts for their enigmatic behaviour, difficulty in catching and ability to disappear. Generally, however, mullet provide great sport for the sea angler. To make the most of your mullet fishing, try the following tips:

• *In most cases, all you will need is freshwater fishing gear. A typical match float rod or quiver tip rod is the ideal, paired with a medium-sized fixed-spool reel. A selection of floats, swim feeders, five- to six-pound line and hooks between size ten and fourteen will complete the job.*

• *Harbours are one of the most reliable places to look for mullet. They get used to feeding on scraps thrown to them by tourists or slivers of fish and guts from the trawlers. Try them with bread or fish titbits.*

• *Sewage outfalls – not necessarily pleasant places to fish – are also very productive. Try float fished maggot or worm.*

• *Mullet will also travel quite a way into freshwater up the estuary. Try ground baiting quite heavily with maggots and casters. Sometimes, floating bread will be taken from the surface.*

• *Explore rocky headlands and bays, especially where the water is relatively shallow and the feeding is rich. Mullet will also travel up creeks once the tide floods in.*

• *Always wear Polaroids, especially if the water is clear, so that you can see fish and gauge how deep they are feeding. Most mullet will take somewhere between the surface and mid-water, but there are times when legering or swim feeding will pick them up off the bottom.*

• *I've found warm, sunny weather to be particularly productive, although overcast days will also work if they are calm.*

• *The peak of the season is from May to October, although you'll find some fish early and late.*

• *If nothing works, try small, silver spinners, perhaps with the hook points tipped with ragworm. Failing that – if you've got the gear – small gold head nymphs fished on fly gear can be spectacularly successful.*

• *Mullet are very easily scared so your approach is vital, especially when they are not used to human activity.*

• *Mullet are spreading; reports suggest that there is barely any coastline from St Ives to the Scottish Isles that aren't visited.*

• *Despite their increasing numbers, return all mullet that are not destined for your cooking pot!*

SECOND-HAND ENGINES

You'll very often give yourself just that extra chance if you can go afloat – not necessarily right out into the ocean but inshore, perhaps exploiting the estuary mouth or harbour. But your boat will need an engine,and sometimes it's a good idea to buy a second-hand one rather than lashing out a lot of money – especially if times are tight or you're not quite sure whether boat fishing is for you. The trouble is, how do you sort out a good deal from a disastrous one?

• *Just looking at the engine overall gives a good idea of whether it's been looked after. Is it battered or scratched, for example? Most important, look at the propeller and skeg for any obvious signs of a bad knock.*

• *Next, you've got to take off the engine cover itself and look for any obvious signs of repair. New gaskets are a giveaway, as are the sighting of any nuts that have recently been unscrewed – look out for chipped paint around them.*

• *With the engine securely off, grip the flywheel and try to move it backwards and forwards. There should be no movement at all; if there is, the upper crankshaft bearings are probably worn.*

• *It's very important to run the engine in a tank of water so that you can see it actually working.*

• *Once the engine is running, put it into gear to make sure it runs smoothly under pressure.*

• *While it's in the tank, check that both the forward and reverse gears are working well. Don't rev up or you'll spill the water.*

• *While the engine is running there should be a good flow of water to indicate the water pump is working. After the engine has run for a while, feel the temperature: it will be warm but it shouldn't be hot.*

• *Ask for any receipts of work done; these should be professional.*

• *Check that the tilt and lock mechanism is working – a point that's easily overlooked.*

• *Hold the leg of the engine and move it backwards and forwards. If there is any play, it indicates that the rubber support bushes are worn.*

• *With the engine off, put the gear lever in the forward position, then try to turn the propeller. If the propeller turns, it could be that the rubber shock absorber is stripped or very badly worn.*

• *If at all possible, use the engine for a proper session's fishing. The above checks are all important, but you can't actually beat getting the engine out on a boat, especially if there's a bit of a tide or a breeze about.*

into the gullies and you may be lucky enough to get a fish of between two and seven pounds.

To get to Beachy Head, you need to walk quite a way along the path from the school (look out for access down to the rocks). It will take you a good fifteen to twenty minutes. Always make sure that you keep your eye on the tide if you're fishing the ledge here. Give yourself plenty of time to escape the rising water and make sure your exit point is well marked. The flood tide is particularly productive for bass, which stream in looking for crabs and prawns amongst the rocks.

There's some great charter-boat fishing out of Eastbourne, as there are plenty of wrecks within easy sailing. This is largely because during the war U-boats used to lie in wait as convoys passed by Beachy Head. In fact, some of the sixty-seven local wrecks are situated only seven miles from the town itself. Expect pollack, cod and conger. Good, close-in boat marks include the Chicken Run, Beachy Head Ledge, the Light Open, the Light Tower and Greenlands. Always be aware that there are some strong tides in this area, off Beachy Head in particular, and very long traces of up to twenty feet will often out-fish the standard six-foot trace.

ACCOMMODATION – Eastbourne is a major holiday centre so there's a wide range of accommodation; phone the Tourist Information Centre on 01323 411400.

TACKLE SHOPS – Eastbourne has some excellent tackle shops; phone Tony's Tackle Shop on 01323 731388 or Eastbourne Pier Bait and Tackle on 01323 648322, or try The Angler's Den in Pevensey Bay on 01323 460441

BOAT HIRE – for charter boats, phone Phil Batt on 01424 212602, Roger Wilson on 01323 766076, Nigel Snelling on 01342 712881 or Brian Kent on 01323 762439. My good friend Jim Whippy, editor of the excellent magazine *Boat Fishing*, lives in nearby Pevensey Bay and comments on the wide variety of fish that you can expect to find out from Eastbourne with any one of these skippers. Conger of seventy pounds are not unusual. Also expect some very good thornback. Bream, gurnard, dogfish and bull huss also proliferate and, of course, there are plenty of cod around the wrecks.

SEAFORD AND NEWHAVEN

Seaford and Newhaven have good possibilities, and the latter is a centre for deep-sea fishing. This area offers something just a little bit different – and I'm thinking here of the lighter, more intimate style of sea fishing that you can find in the river estuaries. First of all, let's have a look at the tidal River Cuckmere. You'll find the Cuckmere running towards the sea from the village of Alfriston, which is buried in the pleasant Sussex countryside. Perhaps the best access, however, is to take the A25 a mile out of Seaford heading towards Eastbourne. The river runs under the road itself and you can park by the road bridge. The Golden Galleon pub is nearby with a large car-park, but do avoid busy times for the pub and, as a thank you, always use it afterwards for refreshments!

The river isn't wide – less than fifty yards – so you don't need traditional sturdy sea gear and, in fact, normal freshwater tackle is probably a better bet all round. What can you expect? Well, perhaps the best period of all is from May to early October. During this period you can expect eels, flounder and, most excitingly, bass and mullet. Approaches? Well, for the eels and plaice, why not try float fishing as something different? Of course, light beach gear will also do the trick. For bass, you can spin or try peeler crab, a very popular bait here and

OVERCOMING SEASICKNESS

It could well be that you're looking at your first trip offshore – perhaps just drifting feathers for mackerel, spinning for bass or going a way out to do some codding. Seasickness is always a potential problem, but don't panic. There are ways round it.

• *Until you get your sea legs, don't think about going out on really rough days. Get used to boat fishing in calmer conditions.*

• *Be careful about what you have to drink the night before. It sounds obvious, but if you're feeling queasy to start with, then boat fishing is hardly going to help you.*

• *Watch what you have for breakfast. I always go for a bit of cereal and fruit. Don't overdo the fry-ups; better still, ignore them altogether.*

• *There are all manner of pills, potions and wristbands on the market designed to combat seasickness. Perhaps they work, perhaps they don't, but if they give you confidence, then go for it. A lot of seasickness is undoubtedly psychological!*

• *Don't sit next to the engine – the smell and the noise can prove a problem. Equally, if in doubt, move away from any potential grim spots, such as where the rubby-dubby is being prepared.*

• *Keep yourself occupied – talk to the skipper or take binoculars so that you can watch out for seabirds and other sea life.*

• *If you think you're going to be in trouble, concentrate on the horizon for a while – this gives you a point of reference.*

• *Try never to look down when you're tying knots or undoing tangles. This is especially important in a swell.*

everywhere. You'll probably find that the first couple of hours of both the flood and the ebb suit the bass well, and always look out for any signs of feeding fish.

Now to the mullet. These really do swarm in huge numbers up the Cuckmere, and there are some big fish. You can often find them at low water, when the flow is at its lowest and the fish congregate in the deeper pools. However, when the water is rising, expect to see them following the water line, feeding very close in, hungry for food. The problem here, as everywhere, is that the mullet's natural diet is almost impossible to imitate. Therefore, you've got to wean them onto something that you can put on a hook. Bread is very much a favoured bait and the mullet here have seen enough of it to know what it is. However, you would be very wise to ground bait with it liberally and not simply use a piece on the hook. Mix a loaf or two into a bucket with plenty of water so that it's good and sloppy, but don't make it too soft – you need to throw it out ten yards or so. You can also put in some flavourings – especially fish oils – to throw off a good scent.

There's no doubt that float fishing is by far the best method of approach for these fish. Use a twelve- or thirteen-foot freshwater float rod with an Avon-type float capable of carrying enough lead for you to cast to where the fish are. A single SSG will often do. For the hook bait, it's best to experiment. Sometimes the mullet will like a big piece of flake on a number six hook. At other times, they'll want just a shred of bread on a size fourteen. You're best fishing light – a four- or five-pound line is quite enough – and use it straight through to the hook. Don't try to stop the mullet in its first run but be prepared to give it line – you shouldn't find too many snags about.

To find the second venue in this area, the River Ouse, carry on down the A259 into Newhaven. In the centre, turn north on the Kingston road and look for the signpost to Piddinghoe. You'll find the village after about a mile and a half, and there's plenty of parking available. The river at this point is some way from the open sea and you'll find the same range of species as in the Cuckmere, but with one extra attraction – there is always the chance of sea trout between May and September. This is one of our most glamorous fish species and, although they're not plentiful, it's always worth taking a spinning rod. If you see any surface activity, it's a good idea to investigate it with a little silver spoon. Every year, some very good specimens are taken.

Sea fishing isn't always about big open beaches, rocky headlands or charter-boat wreck fishing – some of the most exciting stuff round our shores can be as intimate as the sport offered on the Ouse and Cuckmere.

THE ELUSIVE TRIGGER FISH

If you catch a dramatic looking fish that's as deep as it is long, and rather looks like a dinner plate with fins, then the chances are you've picked up a trigger fish. Once they were very rare, but over the last ten years or so warmer conditions have seen a good increase in their numbers.

• *They tend to stick to the south and south-west coasts.*

• *You'll be surprised how well they fight given their shape. Don't expect a tireless battle but be prepared for short, aggressive runs.*

• *They aren't particularly large fish – be pleased with a two-pounder and be very proud of anything over three.*

• *They are almost exclusively a warm-water fish, so you needn't bother looking for them before August or after October.*

• *Look for them well out of the force of strong currents. They prefer slack water and tend to shelter away from a fast flow.*

• *They have a small mouth, but one that's full of tiny, sharp teeth. Their jaws are very powerful, for crushing the shellfish that form the major part of their diet.*

• *Take care of that sharp dorsal fin when you're handling a trigger fish. To depress it, simply press the second spine of the fin and you'll find that that dagger-like first fin folds neatly down. In fact, you are actually 'triggering' the action!*

• *Trigger fish tend to move in quite large shoals, so if you catch one, there are often more following on behind.*

• *For bait, try mackerel strips, ragworm tipped with squid, or peeler crab.*

◫ **ACCOMMODATION** – contact the Seaford Tourist Information Centre on 01323 897426 or the Newhaven Tourist Information Centre on 01273 483448.

◯ **TACKLE SHOPS** – try the Newhaven Angler on 01273 512186.

BRIGHTON

Brighton is the next major centre and boasts a tremendous marina for the angler. It is clean and safe, and offers up wonderful catches. The Marina Village is situated at the eastern end of the seafront and offers plentiful parking. Both arms of the marina are run by Dave Grinham, who operates to the highest possible standard. The toilets are immaculately cared for and the place is safe for children and novices alike. Day tickets are cheap and plenty of thought has been put into the whole operation.

It is the spectacular bass that makes the fishing so special in the area. There have been lots of double-figure fish landed in recent years, including one of seventeen and a half pounds. There are also plenty of mackerel and garfish for youngsters throughout the summer months, and you'll also find mullet, pollack and wrasse. There are plenty of flatfish and, in autumn, big catches of whiting and codling are taken on the night tides.

⊨ ACCOMMODATION – phone the Tourist Board in Brighton on 09067 112255 for details of accommodation in the area.

○ TACKLE SHOPS – Brighton Marina boasts an excellent tackle shop, The Tackle Box on 01273 696477.

WORTHING AND LITTLEHAMPTON

Worthing offers excellent beach and pier fishing and there's some good mixed catches from boats. The River Adur is also worth checking out for flounders and mullet in the summer months.

Finally, we come to the port of Littlehampton, once known as the capital of black bream fishing. Although it passed into the wilderness for a while, the bream are now returning. There is a far-sighted and enlightened policy of catch and release, so the stocks are protected and flourishing.

But there's far more to Littlehampton than bream. It offers very varied fishing indeed – everything from tope and conger through to plaice and ray. One species that is becoming increasingly common is the undulate ray, and some cracking specimens are being located. Another bonus is that Littlehampton enjoys the protection afforded by Selsey Bill to the west. In fact, conditions for the shore and boat angler only really become impossible when the wind goes round to the south east. There is plenty for the shore angler to enjoy in the area, and the upper reaches of the estuary produce great bass and mullet fishing, with plenty of flounder available. Throughout the summer, there is good mackerel and garfish, along with flatfish and bass. Selsey Bill, itself, is a prime mark for smooth-hound during the summer.

⊨ ACCOMMODATION – phone the Tourist Information Centre in Worthing on 01903 210022 or Littlehampton on 01903 713480.

○ TACKLE SHOPS – in Worthing, phone Ken Dunman on 01903 239802 and Prime Angling on 01903 821594. The top tackle shop in Littlehampton is the Tropicana on 01903 715190.

⬅ BOAT HIRE – phone M. Pratt on 01798 342370 or S. Hipgrave on 01903 691697. The full list can be obtained from the Harbour Master on 01903 721215.

SEA-FISHING SITES IN HAMPSHIRE & DORSET

'This is a great boat-fishing area, especially around the Solent. I just tend to work the west, often very close to the Needles, but working offshore during the summer. There's a huge variety of fish to be caught and something for everybody, no matter what the season. The cod, of course, are something special – the biggest I've ever had on my boat is forty-two pounds, but twenty- and thirty-pounders aren't at all uncommon. I run a competition every year for the biggest cod to come onto my boat. I put up £200, and it's invariably a big fish that takes the money. It just adds a little bit of spice to everybody's day I guess, and is regarded as a bit of fun. It does show the stamp of the fishing that we have on offer here, however.'

DAVE STEPHENSON, A SKIPPER OFF YARMOUTH

Dave is a man of huge experience in this area and he quite obviously loves what is on offer. The black bream fishing is absolutely superb, especially during the spring and summer months. Dave suggests using a ten-pound line for these game and very attractive fish. After all, what's the point of using tackle so heavy that you don't feel the true excitement of the fight? My very first taste of sea fishing came at Mudeford, years and years back. I was fishing for flatties in Christchurch Bay. They were only up to a pound or so, but provided great sport on the light gear I was using. However, I couldn't come to grips with the vast shoals of grey mullet that I saw. They were simply beyond me, far too cunning, far too finicky. Mind you, forty years on, I'm not sure that I still have any hard and fast recipes for success! Southampton Water offers some very intriguing estuary fishing, and flounders are very common. However, in the summer, mullet, mackerel, bass and all manner of other species abound. The Solent is also a very interesting site for tope. In short, this portion of the English south coast is a tremendous area offering some superb possibilities.

HAMPSHIRE & DORSET

THE SOLENT

For the best opportunities, get yourself afloat in the Solent. There are all manner of marks, and the relative shelter afforded by the mainland and the Isle of Wight means that it is rare for trips to be cancelled. There's sport all the year round and endless species to be targeted. Historically, the Solent offers some very big cod, especially from the late autumn onwards. Expect fish of twenty or even thirty pounds. Get them on big baits – squid is a favourite and so, too, is pirking. There are cod in the summer, and you'll probably find them close to the wrecks. Expect big pollack, too, along with conger and ling.

In summer, the Solent is an absolute treasure trove for those interested in smaller sporting species such as bass and black bream. Fish for these comparatively light and you are in for a really magnificent time. The tope fishing can be tremendous and you will also find several species of ray, as well as smooth-hound. Selsey Bill, at the eastern end of the Solent, is particularly noted for tope and smooth-hound.

The Nab and the Needles are two of the top marks – you'll find Lymington boats fishing the Needles, and the Langstone fleet heading for the Nab. There's some controversy amongst local anglers as to which is the better area – the Needles to the west or the Nab to the east. Both areas are quite fabulous and offer superb possibilities – especially for winter codding, which is perhaps the prime fishing of all.

There isn't a huge amount of interesting ground around the Needles. In fact, the top marks to the south east are comparatively featureless. The bottom is certainly very flat, with only infrequent rough patches to break it up. There are some very shallow gullies where the cod are known to feed, but you will need a skilful skipper to locate these. You don't catch great numbers of cod off the Needles, but there are plenty for everybody and they are of a very good size – certainly more big fish come from the Needles than the Nab.

The Nab, however, does have an enthusiastic following and it's not hard to understand why. The Nab area is environmentally more exciting to fish and there is a real range and variety of sport there. Nevertheless, perhaps because the cod are more grouped, blanks are arguably more common than they are around the Needles. However, both areas offer great sport, which can be accessed with skippers of huge experience.

There are all sorts of bonuses in the summer. I've already mentioned the black bream fishing, but you will also come across some great conger fishing. There are plenty of fish in the fifty-pound mark and a lot of these are free swimming, so you can enjoy the fight and not worry about lugging them away from the wrecks.

⊨ **ACCOMMODATION** – for accommodation in the Solent area, phone the Southampton Tourist Information Centre on 02380 221106.

○ **TACKLE SHOPS** – Paiges Fishing Tackle, Hayling Island on 02392 463500 is a mine of information on the best skippers, best tackle and best methods in the area.

🡆 **BOAT HIRE** – if you want to try fishing the Needles, contact the skipper of *Challenger* on 01425 619358. Ron Bundy on 01425 629776 offers wreck and reef fishing, along with shark and other exotica! Tuition is also available. Dave Stephenson, out of Yarmouth on the Isle of Wight, on 01983 821225, also has a great reputation. The Lymington fleet is extensive, but try Arthur Savage on 02380 897111 for starters.

THE ISLE OF WIGHT

My limited trips to the Isle of Wight have all proved hugely successful. There's just so much sea fishing around that great experience isn't necessary, especially as there are so many good skippers and tackle shops willing to give advice for the newcomer.

One of my own favourite spots is Ventnor, situated on the south of the island. The western end of the beach there often proves a favourite, with some good bass, skate and conger about.

I don't know what it is about feathering for mackerel, but I'm invariably beaten by everyone around me, no matter how inexperienced they are. This can be an extremely humiliating experience, but you've got to wear it with good grace! What it does show is that mackerel fishing really offers good sport for everyone and I can't think of a better way of getting kids, especially, interested.

If you're not after a great number of fish, my own tip is to sally out with really light gear and perhaps a single feather. If you're using an ultra-light spinning rod, a mackerel of a couple of pounds will give you exhilarating sport. Far better than just winching them in on tackle fit for a tope.

Close by, just to the east, is the tiny village of Bonchurch with its excellent rock marks. Conger and bass feature heavily here.

Moving west from Ventnor, you come to the long, western stretch from Blackgang to Freshwater Bay – an intriguing area for all manner of species. Ray, conger and bass are the target species here throughout the summer and into the autumn. Top marks feature the Brighstone end of Atherfield, somewhere between the holiday camp and Dutchman's Point. Expect conger and bass – the former often going to forty pounds or so. Great sport.

The area around St Catherine's Point, just to the east of Blackgang, offers a whole complex of ledges and gullies generally best looked at when the water is low and plans can be formulated. Always be aware of rising tides, however, and make sure you've got a good exit in mind.

The piers of the island at Yarmouth, Ryde and Sandown all fish extremely well. Sandown is particularly notable for good painted ray, and you will find cod putting in an appearance as autumn draws on. Yarmouth can also produce some surprise species – for example, you may find the occasional good stingray.

Cowes is a long-time favourite for flounder fishermen, all along the River Medina that runs from Newport down to Cowes Harbour. You'll probably find the best sport in the early autumn – October would be my choice. Some local knowledge is well worth seeking out as the shoals do move around according to the season and the state of the tide.

Fish are of a good average size, however, and you'll also see plenty of mullet on the move, along with school bass. It's an area that you can target successfully with freshwater gear. How about float fishing with small worms and lines of around five to six pounds breaking strain? You'll also pick up small silver eels to boot. As for Cowes Harbour, expect to see some staggering mullet. Once again, you can expect flatfish (including sole), along with some decent bass.

My old fishing partner, John Nunn, began his teaching career down in the Isle of Wight and his tales of the splendours of Bembridge inspired me to make the occasional visit. I'm glad I did. The number of species to be caught there is endless – conger, ling, bream, turbot, bass, brill, skate, ray, pollack... and that's not mentioning the countless sizeable mullet that drift around the harbour.

There's shark fishing available, too, during the high summer months, along with tremendous mackerel fishing for the more fainthearted! Top areas include the shore from White Cliff to Bembridge, which combines rock and shingle – perfect for both bass and conger. Near the Crab and Lobster Inn there's a sand gully that can be accessed from nearby rocks.

If you can get out to the Bembridge Ledge early in the year, you can expect good bream, along with the mackerel. And those mullet in Bembridge Harbour are big enough to make your eyes water. Mind you, they're very canny and exceptionally wary of heavy gear.

I'm very aware that I've only scraped the surface of the tremendous fishing that the Isle of Wight has to offer, but I hope I've given a sample of the sport that the visitor can hope to expect. As a holiday venue for the whole family, it is unsurpassed.

ACCOMMODATION – the island is very attractive, easily accessed by ferry, and offers the visitor a wide range of accommodation. Contact the Tourist Information Centres at Ventnor, Shanklin, Sandown, Cowes and Ryde for details. All have the same telephone number: 01983 813818.

FISHING FOR COD

All along the south coast, big cod continue to come inshore during the autumn and winter. However, despite the gloomy forecasts of the fishery scientists, good cod are there to be caught throughout the summer, especially if you take a charter boat out to the more distant offshore wrecks. These will be situated at least twenty miles out, with most of the really good marks being found at thirty-plus miles. Cod can generally be caught from the end of April right through to August, but it's best to contact an experienced skipper who is aware of their comings and goings. Cod are very mobile fish indeed, and you've got to keep a tag on their movements. The following tips may help:

• A good fish finder is absolutely essential for pinpointing the shoals. Don't expect them to be present at the same point day after day. Look for clumps of fish showing close to the bottom.

• Pirks are generally considered the most 'killing' method. However, in recent years, modern, plastic lures have become more and more popular. The main reason for this is that they can be fished with leadheads to get them down deep and direct to the bottom. Their fluid, fluttering movement can also prove absolutely irresistible.

• The Twin Tail is a particular 'killer' – go for it in electric shades of red and orange.

• Be prepared to change both the size of the Twin Tail and the amount of lead needed according to the state of the tide. You want to get the Twin Tail down deep as quickly as possible, but you don't want such a heavy lead that the action is masked.

• Work the Twin Tail with a jigging-type action once it hits the bottom.

• Over very rough ground, or in heavy tides, it pays to wind the lure rather than jig it – you lose fewer rigs and have better control.

• Smaller Twin Tails often work well for bass and other bonus species. For bass, let the lure flutter around in the tide. Use as light a leadhead as you can get away with.

• Twin Tails aren't the only plastic lures available. The originals were Redgills and they can still prove a real winner if fished properly. Also, try different coloured shads and jellyworms.

• Contact Fishtek on 01647 441020 for all the latest in plastic lures. The Harris Angling Company also offers a huge selection; you can contact them on 01692 581208 for all the latest advice on some tremendous products.

○ TACKLE SHOPS – with such great fishing, there are tackle shops aplenty: Stuart's Bait and Tackle in Shanklin on 01983 868100 and in East Cowes on 01983 280985, Scotties in Newport on 01983 522115 and in Sandown on 01983 404555, The Screaming Reel in Ryde on 01983 568745, and the Tacklebox at Totland Bay on 01983 752260.

⛵ BOAT HIRE – contact Chris Solomon in Bembridge on 01892 874100, or Dave Stephenson, skipper of the *Becky M*, in Yarmouth on 01983 821225.

LYMINGTON AND BEAULIEU

Lymington offers some exotic fishing for tope, stingray and big bass. However, I personally have had most of my fun at Beaulieu, a little way up the estuary. This is a mark with a great deal of history about it, situated as it is so close to the great house of Beaulieu. It's a tremendous area for a family holiday – Beaulieu itself offers everything children need for a couple of days, and there are always the ponies of the New Forest.

There are plenty of flatfish about, but what particularly attracts me to the area is the tremendous mullet fishing. You can expect some bass as well, but the mullet really flock here. And what mullet they are – shoals and shoals of really good fish.

As always with this enigmatic species, catching them can be another matter altogether. I've done particularly well on one or two occasions with maggots and then failed with them completely just a day or two later. Tiny worms – either portions of rag or even small redworms – have also done well from time to time. I've caught the odd fish on tiny silver spinners with the hooks tipped with pieces of worm, too. What I've always tried to do is get the mullet going on mashed bread. This has happened for me once or twice around the countryside, but never, so far, at Bucklers Hard.

It's fascinating fishing when you can achieve a breakthrough – just watching the shoals of three- to five-pound fish ploughing into the bread, slurping it from the surface before the gulls can get it. Float fish a piece of flake some eighteen inches down along with the current through the area. Bites are rapid, and, it's got to be said, frequently difficult to hit.

All in all, this is a terrific place for some summer fishing and plenty of fun for all the family.

⊨ ACCOMMODATION – accommodation is abundant. Phone the Southampton Tourist Information Centre on 02380 221106.

○ TACKLE SHOPS – contact Forest Sports, Milford on Sea, Lymington, on 01590 643366.

⚜ TICKETS – tickets for Beaulieu can be obtained from the Harbour Master, Bucklers Hard, on 01590 616200 or from the Estate Office, Beaulieu, on 01590 612345.

⛵ BOAT HIRE – contact Ted Entwistle in Beaulieu on 02380 845272.

POOLE

Poole offers a huge amount for the holidaying angler. It's a top tou
destination with plenty of activities to keep the non-fishing membe
of the family interested. There's good beach and quay fishing in the
natural harbour. However, the place has really taken off when it com
to charter fishing. You don't have to go too far out to find some terrifi
opportunities and the inshore marks fish very well indeed – especially
with a light line approach.

The reefs off Poole are home to a wide variety of species and there are
plenty of black bream and pollack during the summer. The sandbanks
and ridges are also excellent for members of the ray family and you can
have good sport with small-eyed, blonde and undulate if the conditions
are kind. Old Harry Rocks is a well-known mark, and if your skipper
knows his stuff, he'll be able to point you in the right direction for some
very good bass fishing. It's also a top area for tope.

Holes Bay Road in Poole is one of the top shore marks, and is easily
accessible for the visiting angler. This is a real hotspot for flounder, from
October right through to the later part of the winter. You'll also pick up
mullet and bass during the summer. The area is muddy at low tide, but it
fishes particularly well on the flood. If possible, try and get there in the
evening. The area is skirted by a dual carriageway that offers no parking,
so you will have to park in the centre and walk. It will take you fifteen to
twenty minutes, but it's well worth the effort.

🛏 ACCOMMODATION – contact the Tourist Information Centre in Poole on 01202 253253.

⚪ TACKLE SHOPS – for good local advice, contact Poole Sea Angling Centre on 01202
676597, A C Angling on 01202 734451, Castaways on 01202 739202 or Dick's on 01202
679622.

🚤 BOAT HIRE – contact skipper Mike Taylor on 01202 687200 to arrange a trip on his
boat, the *Just Mary*. Poole Sea Angling Centre on 01202 676597 organises a great
deal of charter fishing. Or, try Sea Fishing Limited on 01202 679666 for bass trips and
deep-sea expeditions.

WEYMOUTH

Weymouth is a quaint coastal town and very much a top holiday area in
the south of England. So, once again, this is a perfect venue for the sea
angler setting out with the family. But, above all, Weymouth is really
becoming well-known for its exceptional charter fleet. It offers Channel
Island trips and wrecking, reef and bank fishing for groups or
individuals. The Weymouth Conger Festival is also something that has

HAMPSHIRE

RSET

What makes a good charter-boat skipper? If you're new to an area or on holiday, what are the things to look out for once you're afloat? After all, a skipper can absolutely make or break your day.

• *Generally, a really good skipper will have been, or is, an angler himself. Only then can he really understand what an angler actually wants.*

• *The good skipper makes you welcome. He's not surly or secretive but open and fun. You know instinctively that it will be good to spend the day with him. After all, you are his guests and you deserve the best.*

• *A good skipper will go that extra mile and really put himself out in every way just to make sure that his guests have a really splendid day.*

• *A good boat will often have a really good crewman – the sort of person who's always there to sort out tangles with the net or offer a cup of tea.*

• *A good skipper won't simply rest on his laurels if a fish or two is caught. If sport dries up, he'll up-anchor three or even four times a day in a constant effort to find the fish that his clients want.*

• *The modern skipper will be good with electronics, able to read his screens and know exactly where to put the boat.*

• *But there is more than simple electronic gadgets to a good skipper's armoury. He'll have that real, solid bank of experience so that he knows exactly where to put a boat to fish a wreck. A GPS screen can only show you so much.*

• *Conservation will be a vital issue to the good, modern skipper. He won't dream of killing any fish unnecessarily and he certainly wouldn't gaff congers, for example. Rather, he would use a T-bar to make unhooking easy. Around Hayling, for example, skippers will never kill a smooth-hound – something common only a few years back. The best skippers have very large landing nets, virtually always home-made, that are capable of taking a forty-pound tope or a fifty-pound conger. That way, they can be taken from the sea safely, weighed, unhooked and put back without any damage being done to their internal organs.*

• *A good skipper will have a sound reputation around the harbour or in the tackle shops.*

• *The good skipper will be the one who has survived and has a long history. It's good to check, if you can, just how long he's been in the job.*

• *You can't do better than buy* Boat Fishing *monthly. This is a tremendous magazine and really pinpoints some of the best skippers around our shores. An excellent starting point.*

become a major talking point among anglers. The first Weymouth Open Conger Competition took place in 1994 and it's now an important date in the diary of any angler who seeks big eels.

The whole concept of the festival is encouraging. First of all, it's run over three days, so luck plays very little part indeed. Competitors also fish with the skipper of their choice – this is a great idea, for it means the skipper becomes an integral part of what's going on. Teamwork becomes more and more important, and catches certainly benefit.

What I like the most about the competition, though, is the huge amount of thought that goes into conserving the eels. For example, the skippers keep in constant contact with each other over the radio so that only the very biggest eels, the potential winners, have to go through the ordeal of being weighed. For the rest, the skippers make their own assessment and keep score. This means that the vast majority of eels can be brought to the boat and unhooked with very little risk of harm. For example, the 2001 competition saw 802 conger caught with 790 being returned alive – that's a huge percentage, one that would have been inconceivable just a few years ago.

As I've said, it's the skippers that really run the competition. It's up to them to find the bait – generally mackerel. Then they've got to make the right choice over the target wreck. This isn't always easy, especially with the amount of commercial fishing in the area. The state of the tide has got to be taken into account, as you need to anchor up to fish successfully for eels. Any drifting and you're in trouble. The logistics take some working out – for example, the tides, the wrecks, steaming time, fishing time – so the competition is really organised like a military campaign. In short, it's a good job that the skippers have a very good grasp of what this type of fishing is all about. There are many good people to contact (see overleaf).

If you're serious about conger fishing then it's a good idea to consider joining the British Conger Club (BCC). They have a lively AGM, an annual conger festival, a yearbook and three newsletters a year. Best of all, you will be a part of a group of like-minded individuals and be able to swap information on tackle, baits, methods and the best places to find your favourite fish.

To get into the club, you have to catch either a conger of twenty-five pounds plus from the shore, over thirty pounds from a reef or over forty pounds if you're wreck fishing. You don't have to kill the fish, you just need the signatures of two independent witnesses. There are over 1,500 members of the club. The BCC is a very right-minded organisation and is passionately committed to the conservation of these fascinating fish. They do a lot of tagging, which gives valuable insights into the movements of conger.

⊨ **ACCOMMODATION** – phone the Tourist Information Centre on 01305 785747.

○ **TACKLE SHOPS** – contact the Anglers Tackle Store on 01305 782624, Weymouth Angling Centre on 01305 777771 or Reels and Deals on 01305 787848.

➤ **BOAT HIRE** – the conger competition was first devised by Pat Carlin and Chris Caines, and their boats *Channel Chieftain* and *Tiger Lily* are well worth investigating; contact them on 01305 787155 and 01305 821177 respectively. Another top name is Paul Whittall; his boat, *Off Shore Rebel IV*, saw the capture of the winning conger for 2001 – a magnificent ninety-pound specimen; contact Paul on 01305 783739. There are fourteen skippers in all making up the charter fleet, so go along and really get into those big eels.

CHESIL BEACH

Moving further westwards, we come to the rightly famous Chesil Beach that leads out to the isle of Portland. Chesil runs for seventeen miles from West Bay, near Bridport, right out to Portland, and the pebbles steadily increase in size as you move from west to east. It is incredibly scenic and offers a huge range of opportunities. For holidaymakers, a base at Abbotsbury can hardly be bettered. It is central for Chesil Beach and offers some great shore fishing. The village and environs are incredibly picturesque, with perfect Dorset thatched cottages. You'll find a large car-park on the road signed 'To the beach' and a wooden walkway will take you right up to the top of the shingle. There's a café and toilets to cater for your every need. To get here, take the road out of Weymouth and follow the signs for Portland. It generally pays to walk some distance from the crowds. Keep on the move for fifteen to twenty minutes and you'll usually be pretty much on your own. The area is fairly featureless, but the water is deep close in and the abundance of species makes for exciting fishing.

Where do you begin... trigger fish, pout, mackerel, dogfish, whiting, bull huss, cod and dab, smooth-hound, plaice, garfish, mullet, gurnard and the odd conger eel – they're all there.

Many of the locals like float fishing here, especially for garfish, bass and mackerel – the latter can be very, very prolific. You'll pick up plenty of high-quality plaice and dab on the bottom, along with trigger fish, which are a brilliant species. If you haven't tangled with them yet, it's well worth making the effort (see page 42). They seem to go for crab or ragworm, with squid also proving popular.

Calm sunny weather is generally favoured in the summer, especially for the mackerel. Autumn is a good time. After the school holidays, the whole area quietens down and whiting begin to appear in numbers. If you walk eastwards towards Portland from the beach, you will come to the Dragon's Teeth – generally considered one of the top marks for cod. These are, in fact, a series of concrete slabs created as tank traps during the war.

At any time of the year be careful of strong south-westerlies, as the undertow makes the shingle very unstable indeed.

Let's now move to the extreme western end of Chesil Beach, to the picturesque town of West Bay with its idyllic, little Dorset harbour. This, again, is a perfect holiday area, but do be aware that it can get very busy during the summer as there are several caravan parks and campsites around. Shore fishing abounds – the promenade and harbour wall are generally favoured, from the summer right through to October. Mackerel, garfish, scad and wrasse are all plentiful. You'll also pick up dogfish and bass in good conditions. Mullet fishing around the harbour can be brilliant, with both thin-and thick-lipped mullet around. Four-pounders are quite common and you will see fish of six pounds or, occasionally, above. This is one place where you really can get them going on bread.

The East Beach is also a top shore mark and is found on the Portland side of the harbour. It's really a steep shingle bank with lots of rubble on the bottom. There's an offshore reef, which can just be reached by long casting. There are some very big plaice around – certainly two-pounders – and after dark you stand a chance of catching bass up to that magical ten-pound mark. Lug and rag both work well, especially tipped with a piece of sand eel or mackerel. Midway along the beach, you will come to Port Coombe, which is the local name for the very obvious cliff. You'll pick up all the species already mentioned. In the winter, the area also produces some half-decent cod fishing. The best results come at the top of the tide, especially around the half-light, either morning or evening.

West Bay also offers some really good boat-fishing opportunities. There are half a dozen or so charter boats working out of the town during the summer months, of which a couple fish the wrecks for cod, ling, pollack and conger. You'll also meet up with some really good bass fishing. There's even a limited amount of shark fishing on request. Reef fishing is the other option, particularly for the excellent bream fishing from midsummer onwards. You will find conger and pollack, along with bull huss, wrasse, dogfish and ray.

Overall, the whole area of Chesil Beach is a magnet for sea anglers, whatever their favourite species. It's a great place for the family holiday, but be aware that it's always a busy area during the summer. Providing you don't mind this too much, get yourself there as quickly as possible.

ACCOMMODATION – there's a wide range of accommodation – phone the Bridport Tourist Information Centre on 01308 424901.

TACKLE SHOPS – the West Bay Angling Centre on 01308 421800 and the Tackle Shop on 01308 423475 offer information, bait, tackle and access to the charter boats.

BOAT HIRE – contact Geoff Clarke 01308 425494 or Chris Reeks on 01460 242678.

FLOAT FISHING

Float fishing has long been popular along the rocky coastline of the West Country and around the Channel Islands. It's an attractive form of fishing and provides lots of advantages over traditional legering methods. To get the most out of float fishing, follow these tips:

• *You can only use floats under certain conditions and at certain times of the year. There would be little point, for example, trying to cast out a float eighty yards on a winter's night into a raging surf!*

• *Top species to pursue with a float include garfish, mackerel, wrasse, mullet, flounder, bass and sometimes pollack. Obviously, floats are of little use for big, deep-living species such as conger.*

• *A basic float technique is to use a small pike float sliding up and down the main line with the depth set by a stop-knot. Make sure you put on a drilled bullet big enough to cock the float. Use it with a light carp rod and eight- to ten-pound line so that you can cast the rig a decent way.*

• *Set the float to around about four feet to begin with. You can readjust it during the course of the day.*

• *Bait up with fish strips, prawn, crab or ragworm.*

• *It will help if you can ground bait around the float. Or attach a swim-feeder onto the line under the float and fill it with oil, pieces of fish or anything that has a good odour. An oil-soaked rag is also a good idea. It's a good method for fairly calm conditions from jetties or beaches. It's also excellent employed from a boat.*

• *Simply let the float drift around, and strike as soon as it goes under.*

• *You can also spin using a float – simply put a float on the line above your spinner. This is particularly useful when you're targeting fish, such as mullet, that swim mid-water or just under the surface.*

• *Light floats are particularly excellent for estuaries.*

• *Use floats such as traditional Avons and Wagglers with six-pound line.*

• *Pay some attention to your shotting patterns. Put most of your shot around midway between float and hook with another shot near the hook if you find you're tangling during the cast.*

• *Visibility can be a problem. Red and orange are favourite colours, but you'll also find black stands out very well under many conditions.*

• *Perhaps you fancy night fishing with a float. Go to your tackle shop and ask for a Drennan-type float with a starlight isotope to put into the insert at the top. Depending on the power of the isotope, you can see a float anything up to twenty-five yards away under most conditions.*

Ships at anchor in the summertime are an ideal fishing venue for mullet as they browse the sheltered water looking for titbits of food. Try a piece of slow-falling breadflake.

Old Harry Rock, off Poole in Dorset, is one of the best-known landmarks along the English south coast. It's a terrific spot for fishing throughout the year.

Lynmouth harbour, in Devon, is a bustling place that sees good runs of summer salmon in the right conditions. You'll also find boats to take you mackerel fishing.

The splendour of the north Devon coast offers great sport for all species at any time of the year. It's not a heavily fished area and you can get away from the crowds.

This fine brace of plaice were taken from a boat. Note the colourful attractor beads on the line that give the bait just that little bit more allure.

St Helier, Jersey

The Channel Islands, which can easily be reached by ferry from Poole, offer some superb sea fishing, really sport-defying superlatives. For those unsure where to target, St Helier, the capital of Jersey, is a must. For a holiday, it is ideal – the family have plenty to entertain them, while the angler can creep away and enjoy him- or herself totally. You can go afloat or you can fish from the harbour walls or the adjacent beaches. Don't forget the duty-free shopping and the lovely weather either. Who can resist the call of the islands when you throw in record ballan wrasse and rays caught from the shore?

The beach fishing is best done either very early or late on, for obvious reasons, but the rewards can be tremendous. The best fishing, right in front of what is called the Gunsight Café, can be mind-blowing. The harbour at St Helier provides a good amount of wall space, and if you're into mullet I doubt whether you will find better fishing anywhere in the world. Mackerel, garfish and bass are also there to be caught. You'll also find wrasse where rocks make up the bottom. Try a sliding float or small spinners. Elizabeth Castle, a sixteenth-century fortress, also provides tremendous sport, with wrasse, pollack, mackerel and garfish, and you'll find some very big eel close in, hiding almost in the foundations. You can expect fish up to fifty pounds!

Most of the locals have their own boats, so there is only a handful of charter boats operating, all based at St Helier. There's wreck, reef and bank fishing and some superb tope on offer. The area is littered with wrecks that produce fantastic cod and pollack. The reefs are well-known for their conger, and black bream are something of a speciality here. The banks offer ray, turbot, bass and brill.

Always take care with the tides at Jersey – they are amongst the biggest in the entire world. This is very important if you should happen to be out in a small boat or fishing from rocks. Also, beware of the sun – you might feel you are in England but, believe me, the rays are much more penetrative.

⊨ **Accommodation** – tourism is what Jersey is all about; contact Jersey Tourism on 01534 500777.

○ **Tackle shops** – contact PJN Fishing Tackle on 01534 874875, JFS Sport on 01534 58195 and I S Marine on 01534 877755.

⇒ **Boat hire** – for charter boats, contact Tony Hurt on 01534 863507 or David Nuth on 01534 858046.

SEA-FISHING SITES IN
SOUTH-WEST ENGLAND

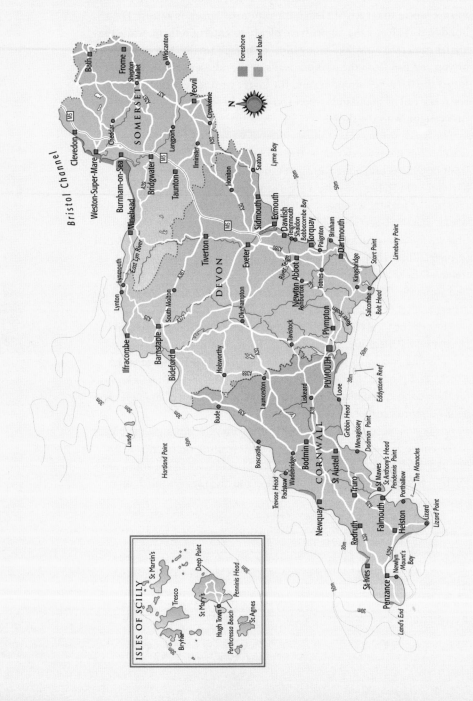

' The sea fishing down here in Devon and Cornwall is, without any shadow of doubt, the best in the country as far as I'm concerned. We've got the best boat fishing by far, and we've got the best shoreline. We've got the best fly rodding; we've got every sea fish that swims, from cod to porbeagle; and there's masses of sheltered water of every description. We've also got Plymouth, a really bustling port with some of the best-developed deep-sea wreck and reef fishing in the country. Take Plymouth Sound, for example – it's not unusual to go out there in a small boat and get amongst twelve different species in a day. It's just incredible. If you ask me, it's an area that's been generally under-publicised for years. Really, if the rest of the world knew what we've got here, we'd be inundated. Add to that some really beautiful coastline, stunning cliffs, great pubs, fantastic accommodation, and you've got a bit of Paradise. '

ROBIN ARMSTRONG, ARTIST, WRITER, FISHERMAN

Robin really is quite correct. There's arguably no other section in this book that offers the quality, quantity and variety that's to be found in the south west. One interesting fact is that a large number of normally freshwater-only anglers turn to the sea when they come down to this area. There are just so many possibilities that every angler wants to try some intimate, hands-on sea fishing – casting heavy weights to the horizon is not the only key to success.

You also have to think about the glorious countryside and coastline when it comes to assessing the fishing in this part of the world. Think of the south Devon coast – the bays, pretty little beaches and snug villages with cosy olde-worlde pubs. Add to that the generally clement weather, and you can see why it's such a popular holiday destination. Stick in your fishing tackle – slightly up-graded freshwater gear is often all you'll need – and join in the fun.

TEIGNMOUTH

The River Teign enters Babbacombe Bay just below Newton Abbot, where it becomes wide and shallow and perfect for summer fishing. It's a haven for sand eels and that means one thing – bass. However, the real draw of Teignmouth is the flounder fishing, which is absolutely legendary. It's traditional winter fishing, but this shouldn't mean the kiss of death for the summer tourist. During the warmer months, mullet, garfish, bass and mackerel are all available. Do remember, though, the rules regarding bass fishing around here – it's designated a nursery area, so boat fishing is not allowed in many areas.

Try Fish Quay at Teignmouth for mullet, though you will need a drop net because of the long haul up from the water. You will find fish around four or five pounds. Mashed mackerel is a favourite ground bait and try a shard of flesh on a small hook under a float. Freshwater hooks tend to be slimmer than sea hooks but still with the requisite power. A size six to twelve is about right. If the fish are very scary, you can go even smaller.

The top end of the estuary is always worth a look. If you press a long way past the road bridge, you will come to the site of a former power station. This is called Newton Quay and it's a favourite place for mullet and flounder in the summer time. Mackerel are also great roamers and will often push a good way upstream – cast small spinners well out into the channel.

Summer flounders are well worth considering. Although they might not be there in the same numbers or size as fish you'll pick up in the winter, you could be in for a real treat towards the end of the summer. You'll pick them up from the well-known winter marks such as Red Rock, Flow Point, Coombe Cellars and Shaldon beach.

⊨ **ACCOMMODATION** – phone Teignmouth Tourist Information Centre on 01626 215666.

○ **TACKLE SHOPS** – get your bait and information from McGeary Newsagents, Northumberland Place, Teignmouth on 01626 7723380.

BRIXHAM BREAKWATER

The fishing continues abundantly as we travel south along Babbacombe Bay through Torquay, Paignton and Brixham. Brixham Breakwater, in particular, is a great summer spot, especially for the tourist. It protects the old fishing port of Brixham from easterly gales and runs about half a mile out into Tor Bay. In the summer, you'll find float fishing works really well for mackerel and garfish. Also, expect a few pollack. It pays to walk at least midway up the breakwater and fish on the outside. The best spot is right at the end at the lighthouse, but watch out for boat traffic. Legering can turn up wrasse and flatfish and, on the inside, in the calm water, you'll find some good mullet, fish up to four or five pounds in weight. If you're up for an early or late session, you can fish for bass or even hope for the odd conger or two. Sand eel is one of the top bass baits here.

One of the nice things about the breakwater is that tides are no real problem. Even the winds are unlikely to trouble you, especially in the summer. However, a very strong easterly will give you problems if you're trying to fish light gear, a float for example, and don't think of going out in an easterly gale. Probably the best time, the locals say, is from two hours before to two hours after high water.

So, this is a perfect place to bring your light, freshwater gear to enjoy some really good fishing with wrasse, mullet, bass and mackerel. Oh, and I'd better warn you – you might see some divers, so beware.

⊨ ACCOMMODATION – contact the Tourist Centre in Brixham on 0906 680 1268 (this is a premium rate number).

○ TACKLE SHOPS – there are two angling shops – the Quay Stores on 01803 853390 and the Angling Centre on 01803 858199. Both shops sell bait and are open year round, including Sundays.

DARTMOUTH

Dartmouth is an area that I have known and enjoyed since childhood. All the usual species are to be found around the river – tremendous mullet and bass, but also some serious conger, along with thornback ray.

However, it is perhaps the boat fishing that people most enthuse about when they talk about Dartmouth. Plaice are to be found in good numbers and size early in the year, with larger ones appearing as the months go past. Try chartering a boat to take you out to the famous Skerries Bank. A knowledgeable skipper is a must to get the best out of the Skerries. It's wrong to think of the flatties being spread around like currants in a cake – they have set lies known only to those who fish regularly.

⊨ ACCOMMODATION – Dartmouth Tourist Information Centre on 0906 680 1268 (this is a premium rate number) will advise on accommodation.

○ TACKLE SHOPS – for further information on fishing in the area, contact Sport 'n' Fish at 16 Fairfax Place, Dartmouth or phone them on 01803 833509.

⬐ BOAT HIRE – Steve Parker is one of the leading skippers hereabouts and he takes parties out to the famous Skerries Bank. Steve is a real expert at locating plaice, not least because he was an angler before becoming a skipper, so he has his priorities well worked out. He can be contacted on 01803 329414.

SALCOMBE

The south west just doesn't come prettier than this. Salcombe is an idyllic, picturesque, bustling little town with a world-famous estuary. In fact, the outer and inner estuaries are possibly the most important small boat angling areas in Britain.

Almost every species is available to be caught in this area. However, once again, note that there is a nursery area for bass: the species may not be targeted upstream from a line between Splat Point and Limebury Point between April 30th and January 1st.

The estuary is particularly noted for turbot and plaice. Between Bolt Head and Mewstone Rock, you will find a very rocky, weedy area that is heavily frequented by wrasse. Five-pounders are common and fish have been landed to seven pounds plus. Don't go too light – this is quick water and it flows over snaggy ground.

You will also find wrasse around the Wharf Rock reef. This is marked by a green buoy and nearby are two patches of rough ground marked by striped navigation pylons.

Plaice and dab abound in the River Salcombe, which is generally held as part of the inner estuary. Once the warm weather arrives, you will find thornback ray and huge numbers of mullet. There's wide availability for hiring your own small boat to whip around the estuary. Alternatively, you may like to join up with one of the charter organisations for some excellent wreck fishing.

Moving further west, we come to the estuary of the River Yealm. This is a truly stunning area, often overlooked by anglers but offering some superb fishing. The estuary is home to good flounder, bass and mullet and you can fish either off the rocks or from beaches.

You'll find that flounder are around throughout the year, but the recognised season runs from early autumn through to the middle of winter. There are also some wrasse, especially around the Old Cellars beach, and they, like the bass and the mullet, are at their most prolific during the summer months.

Access is not difficult and a lot of useful information will be gleaned from the friendly local tackle shops.

ACCOMMODATION – for details of accommodation in the area, contact the Tourist Information Centre in Salcombe on 01722 334956.

TACKLE SHOPS – for all your tackle and bait needs contact Whitestrand Boat Hire on 01548 843818 or Tucker's Boat Hire, Victoria Quay on 01548 842840.

BOAT HIRE – contact Whitestrand Boat Hire or Tucker's Boat Hire on the above telephone numbers.

EDDYSTONE REEF

You'll find Eddystone Reef some fourteen miles or so out of Plymouth. This location has been justly famous for its sea fishing for a century or more and is an all-round brilliant venue. Once upon a time, the Eddystone Lighthouse was manned and the lighthouse keepers who worked there used to tell anglers where the fishing would be at its best. Unfortunately, that's not the case today and you've got to do all the hard work yourself! Experience and skill are necessary to locate the shoals of fish, which – like the lighthouse keepers – are nowadays considerably fewer in number!

So what does this famous mark have to offer? Well, the pollack are legendary, with double-figure fish to be expected at the right time of year – certainly between late spring and the autumn. And if it's not pollack that you're after, the reef still produces some extraordinary bass. Of course, you can winch both species in on any gear you like, but I personally would recommend using sporting gear. Choose either twelve- or sixteen-pound class tackle to get the very best out of pollack. These fish really fight like crazy if you give them half a chance – they are big, beautiful fish and it doesn't do to rush the experience. You'll probably need traces of between fifteen and twenty pounds – say eight feet long in slack water or fifteen feet in full flow. Leads will be around six to eight ounces, but with a weak link – the reef is full of tackle-grabbing snags.

One or two tips – sand eel live bait really do the trick for both bass and pollack. Try catching them on small shrimp-type feathers. Work them on a slow retrieve but don't be in a hurry to strike when you get a take. Continue winding and with any luck the fish will hook itself.

Spring tides are the very best for both pollack and bass at Eddystone.

⊨ **ACCOMMODATION** – the Mount Batten Centre has become the mecca for sea anglers in this part of the world. It offers superb, economically-priced bed and breakfast with a choice of rooms with shared facilities and en suite rooms. There's a brilliant drying room for when you come in all wet and smelly from the sea, freezers for bait and a secure lock-away for all your tackle. The car-park is free and the centre's pontoon is right by the front door so you can tumble onto your charter boat still half asleep. There's a bar, restaurant and good shore fishing all around. Highly recommended for any discerning sea fisherman! For information, phone 01752 404567.

○ **TACKLE SHOPS** – the following are all to be found in Plymouth: Clive's Tackle and Bait on 01752 228940, DK Sports on 01752 662361, Manadon Angling Supplies on 01752 795060, Osborne and Cragg on 01752 223141, The Fishermen's Friend on 01752 606300, The Tackle and Bait Shop on 01752 361294.

🎣 **BOAT HIRE** – a highly recommended skipper in the area is Rob Street, boss of the *Vagabond*. Contact him on 01752 768892 or on his mobile 07770 225160.

FISHING FOR BLUE SHARK

What of the blue shark? The body is streamlined, long and very graceful. The back is blue, merging almost to black, the flanks are paler and the stomach is white. The tail is a main feature, with the upper lobe much longer than the lower one. The fish has two dorsal fins and long, curved pectorals. With this fin arrangement, the blue shark has huge mobility. The teeth are small but, beware, they are strong and ferociously sharp. Given the power of the jaws, the mouth is a formidable killing machine. The skin is rough to the touch and made up of innumerable tiny scales. Shark can look like killers – the 'Jaws of the Deep' – but, like most creatures, the truth belies the fiction. Shark, like all fish, can easily be harmed. Nowadays, nearly all shark are returned, so the days of hauling them over the side of the boat and damaging their internal organs are long gone. To be returned, a shark has to be lifted clear of the water and unhooked without any damage or pressure inflicted on its delicate internal structure.

There are not the numbers of blues left that there once were. Go back to the 1950s and 1960s and you'll be sickened by the old photographs of quayside corpses. The growth rate of blues is slow – around ten pounds a year – so conservation is absolutely essential. Also, remember that the big female you catch is very probably carrying young that will be born in the late spring and early summer. Some females produce twenty or more young. Now that conservation is the watchword, stocks are likely to build up and, who knows, before long multiple catches may occur again.

Tagging is a rewarding conclusion to your fishing. Perhaps that blue has been tagged before and you know someone else has had the pleasure and satisfaction of catching it. By releasing your own blue, this trend will continue. It's also fascinating to see how far round the globe our Cornish blues can wander. It's not unusual for them to turn up in the West Indies!

The blue is a large, hard-fighting species, but don't go over the top with heavy gear or you won't really appreciate the fight. Use sporting tackle for these fish, as you would everything else in the sea. A seven-foot rod in the thirty- to eighty-pound class is about right. You will need a multiplier that can cope with some 400 yards of fifty-pound mono or braid. Pack a butt pad to give you extra leverage and to avoid severe bruising in the abdominal area. It's vital that once a blue is hooked all other anglers reel in and watch the fun. If they don't, the chance of line tangles and a lost fish is immense. Keep mobile around the boat. You'll often have to follow a fish

from one side to the other as the blue nears the boat and shows its
agility. Be careful of going near the bow when the boat has a cabin,
especially if there's a brisk wind and a big swell. Many skippers won't
allow this anyway.

The hook will be large – 10/0s are favoured. The trace will be wire,
200-pound test is not too much, and make sure that it is long. Five or even
six yards is not excessive, as the shark will begin to twist as it comes close to
the boat. Remember those sandpaper-like scales I talked about earlier –
they cut through nylon like a knife.

As for bait, mackerel or herring – providing they are fresh – are hard to
beat. Pilchard can also take fish, as can quite sizeable pollack. The blue
shark will pick up the bait and run with it, rather like a pike in freshwater.
Don't strike at this moment, but once the second run begins, click the
multiplier into gear and strike hard and firm. Some skippers recommend
multiple strikes to set the hook in the hard mouth.

It's usual to fish something between four and six baits from a shark
boat and these are set at different depths, usually supported by balloon
floats. These are easily seen in even rough weather and burst when pulled
under so the taking shark feels no resistance. The baits are set anything
from ten yards or more beneath the surface.

The skill of the skipper is absolutely essential if really good fishing is to
be located. The day's fishing depends on how successful the drift is once the
ground has been reached and the engine cut off. It's possible to fish ten or
more miles during the day, following the tide. It's up to the skipper to know
exactly the best areas for fish and, also, to start up a successful rubby-
dubby trail. This is the crunch time for the fisherman. What has often
seemed a perfect day can turn into a nightmare if you're at all unsure
about your sea legs. The best rubby-dubbies really do smell absolutely foul.
They're often never really changed throughout the season – the skippers
simply top them up with all manner of disgusting fish insides, blood, bran,
pilchards and the devil knows what.

The rubby-dubby trail is absolutely essential to draw the hunting shark
in towards the bait. You'll see it slicking out over the surface of the sea,
almost to the horizon. It's vital that the boat follows this trail and the baits
work within it – all down to the skill of the skipper. Shark hunt very much
by smell, moving up-water towards the rubby-dubby trail and the baits.
Generally, it takes anything up to an hour before the first shark homes in
and the action begins. It's exciting stuff when that balloon begins to race
across the surface.

LOOE AND MEVAGISSEY

Travelling westwards along the south coast of Cornwall, we reach the towns of Looe and Mevagissey, centres famous back in my youth for the first real shark fishing available for the tourist. It was a revelation – the idea that a lad like me could travel down from the north, stay in an idyllic Cornish town and then get out to sea and catch shark, fish bigger than I'd ever clapped eyes on before, or even dreamed possible! Sadly, back in the 1960s, conservation was not an issue, and tremendous harm was done to the stocks. Now, thankfully, a lot more consideration is shown.

Looe's reputation, in particular, is built upon the broad backs of the fabulous blue shark that have inhabited the lower part of the English Channel for so long (see pages 64–5). We have the Atlantic Gulf Stream to thank for their presence here in such great numbers. The first blues begin to arrive early in May, but they're a long way offshore and it's not really until June that the fishing starts in earnest. At this time, you'll find them just twenty or so miles off the Cornish coastline and they're beginning to feed.

Of course, this area has a lot more to offer than just shark, but Looe remains the headquarters of the Shark Angling Club of Great Britain (for details, see below), which was founded way back in 1953. Conservation is now their watchword. Any fish now caught are not hauled onto the boat to be weighed but are instead judged by their length and their girth. Once upon a time, a prospective member of the club had to bring a body back to shore for his or her membership to be accepted. Thankfully, this is no longer the case, and the skipper's decision that the fish weighs a minimum of seventy-five pounds is enough to gain membership.

The shark club has a whole list of recommended skippers, men who really know how to contact the shark and, importantly, how to look after them once they've been hooked.

⊨ ACCOMMODATION – for details of accommodation in the area, contact the Tourist Information Centre in Looe on 01503 262072.

○ TACKLE SHOPS – contact Fishing Shark, Fish Market Quay on 0800 0743554, or the following at The Quay, West Looe: Jack Bray on 01503 262504, Looe Angling Club on 01503 263337 and The Tackle Shop on 01503 262189. In Mevagissey, try Mevagissey Shark Angling, West Wharf on 01726 843430 and Tackle Box, 4 Market Street on 01726 843513.

⊸ BOAT HIRE – you can contact the office of the Shark Angling Club of Great Britain on Looe East Quay anytime between 10:00am and 1:00pm daily. Phone 01503 262646 for a list of the main boats and also general angling information. Just as a rough guide, expect to pay something between £30 and £40 for a day's shark fishing; good value indeed on clean, well-run, safe craft. You can also contact Harry Barnett on 01503 263218 for all information on deep-sea boats. In Mevagissey, skippers can be contacted via Tackle Box on 01726 843513.

BASS ON THE ROCKS

One of the main reasons that bass come in close to feed around rocks is the peeler crab, the soft crab that is shedding its old shell. Crabs begin to peel once water temperatures average 11°C (52°F). Crabs peel on and off from the spring right through towards the autumn.

- Bass love to forage amongst big rocks looking for peeler crabs.
- The rougher the ground, the better. Look for beaches that are mostly rock and boulder with comparatively little sand or gravel.
- Fissured rocks, large boulders, crevices, weed and all similar features are attractive to both crab and bass alike.
- Try putting a crab bait on a piece of sand between rocky areas. The bass will pick it up as they move from one hunting ground to another.
- Look for areas that will hold passing food items. Make a note of pools still full of water at low tide – excellent places. Note the position of weed beds and big boulders lying amongst smaller ones; both are good places.
- Look for deep gullies amongst the rocks and boulders. Bass use these gullies as highways from one feeding area to the next.
- Don't worry too much about depth – the bass will be happy anywhere between three and twelve feet.
- Ask local advice as to the best time to fish because there are simply no hard and fast rules. You might find the best time is one hour before low water and two hours after. Two hours before high water again seems to be good in many areas, but it pays to experiment.
- A good onshore wind tends to increase the number of fish moving in to feed. Don't be afraid of fishing into a good swell, but always ensure your personal safety and don't risk being cut off by a tide.
- Try to use as light a lead as you can get away with. A heavier lead will often snag the bait or pull it down into places the bass can't reach.
- Long casting is often not necessary. A lot depends on how deep the water is in close. If it's over two yards, expect them almost under your rod tip. In shallow water, be prepared to cast fifty to sixty yards.
- For a big bass, use a big hook like a 4/0 or a 5/0 and use the halves from two or three crabs pushed up the shank to make a bait some five or six inches long.
- One of the best methods is a sliding Paternoster.
- Use heavier line than you would think necessary. Twenty-pound breaking strain is a good compromise in really rocky surroundings that can chafe tackle unbelievably.

THE TIP OF CORNWALL

There are many excellent fishing locations in the most westerly part of Cornwall. Falmouth, for example, is a terrific area for both holidays and fishing. There's pier and shore fishing, as well as some great boat opportunities. The Manacle's, Pendennis Point, St Anthony's Head, Porthallow and Lizard are all legendary marks.

Penzance just has to be one of my own favourite areas – beautiful countryside, a pleasant town and some excellent boat, pier and shore fishing. Boat trips can be arranged from the Shell Shop (see below) and you will also find some opportunity for shark fishing.

Why not get away from the bustle a little bit and try Newlyn harbour, just a little south of the main town. Access it on the B3315, just off the A30. Newlyn has a long north pier, where the local trawlers dock, and a shorter south pier, which has a lighthouse. You will find the pier heads are busy during the summer months, but as the light fades, the crowds disperse and the fishing improves. True darkness can give you a good chance of a conger or two. Between May and October, the harbour itself often swarms with mullet. Fish for them light and generally under a float. You will get a lot of information from the Penzance tackle shops (see below).

If it's a fishing and family holiday combined that you're looking for, then it's hard to beat St Ives on the tip of the north Cornish coast. The bay, like the town, is quite wonderful and there's a whole array of fishing possibilities.

⊨ **ACCOMMODATION** – contact the Tourist Information Centre in Falmouth on 01326 312300.

○ **TACKLE SHOPS** – contact the Tackle Box in Falmouth on 01326 315849 for advice on tackle, baits and methods. Or, try Symons in St Ives on 01736 796200. In Penzance, contact Jim's Discount Tackle on 01736 360160, John Wing on 01736 363397 or West Cornwall Angling on 01736 362363.

⇒ **BOAT HIRE** – in Falmouth, contact *Blue Minstrel* on 01326 250352, *Gamgy Lady* on 01326 375458 or Frank Vinnicombe on 01326 372775. In Penzance, boat trips can be arranged from the Shell Shop on 01736 68565. In St Ives, phone the Harbour Master on 01736 795081 or try Symons in the Market Place (see above).

THE ISLES OF SCILLY

The Isles of Scilly, just twenty-eight miles off the coast of Land's End, offer one of the most unexplored areas of fishing around our shores. In fact, to be honest with you, I've never fished there myself. However, the tales that come out of the place are sensational. You've got deep water close inshore and pretty well unexploited fishing. There are four main inhabited islands here and you can get holiday accommodation quite easily. St Mary's is the largest island and possibly offers the most opportunities. There are charter boats available and blue shark are a real speciality here, along with some very big conger. Mind you, there are bound to be endless surprises for anybody who takes the time to explore the area.

Because of the Gulf Stream, spring comes very early indeed and, if the commercial fishermen are to be believed, some big porbeagles move into the area. Rumour has it that there are wrasse everywhere for the shore fisherman, along with conger, dogfish, pollack and mackerel. Areas to concentrate on are Porthcressa beach, Penninis Head and Deep Point. Take my advice – go and explore!

⊨ ACCOMMODATION – the possibilities for holiday accommodation are endless. The Isles of Scilly Tourist Information Centre on 01720 22536 is a mine of information; phone them for brochures and up-to-the-minute advice.

○ TACKLE SHOPS – contact Sports Mode, The Parade, St Mary's, on 01720 422293.

BOSCASTLE AND BUDE

Boscastle in north Cornwall is an absolute dream, the perfect place for the sea angler on holiday. The village is picturesque, the coastline gorgeous and the tiny harbour as cute as anything you'll find anywhere in the world. In short, it's the perfect venue for a holiday in this part of the world. Boscastle is primarily a summer venue too – the Atlantic swells in the winter mean that boat traffic is pretty well nil, so it's the warm months for this super little place.

Boscastle is really the jewel of the north Cornwall coastline, sheltering as it does behind the giant Meachard rock stack that guards the narrow entrance to the harbour. In fact, it's almost fjord-like here, the blue sea twisting and turning amidst high crags. You could almost think that you were in Norway.

There are two main options to pursue when you take a boat out of Boscastle. You can head south past Tintagel Head and along the coast in the direction of Padstow and search out the excellent bass fishing. Alternatively, steam north past Cambeak and Dizzard Point into Bude Bay, where you'll find rough ground, reefs and a whole variety of fish including tope, pollack, black bream, bull huss and, for the guys gunning for the real biggies, even some porbeagles.

Bude Bay really does offer a bit of everything for everybody. You're not fishing far out – just three miles or so from Bude's sandy beaches themselves, but it's a different world out there and you never know what's likely to turn up. A whole variety of baits work – obviously mackerel is

BIG EELS

It's arguable that the south west produces the best conger anywhere around the shores of Britain. The big ports for the enthusiast are Plymouth, Dartmouth, Salcombe and Brixham – all areas where you can pick up really experienced charter-boat captains. As a general rule, you'll be fishing over mid-channel wrecks, often in the shipping lanes.

Conditions are important, and you really need a tide that allows the skipper to anchor his boat just off the wreck so that you can fish a static bait. Conger take their time to pick up food and you won't catch them on the drift. The plan is to put the bait – as often as not a mackerel flapper – on an 8/0, or even a 10/0, as close to the wreck as possible without actually being inside it. Wait for the eel to scent the succulent bait, sidle out and engulf it, and then hit and hold before it gets back to sanctuary. To do this, you're going to need thirty-pound plus tackle. You'll need a 200-pound wire trace – mono-filament will do if it's really, really thick.

Very often, the bigger the conger the more gentle the bite, so be alert. Once you know you've got conger interested, hit it and then the battle really begins. Very often it's tempting to think that you've actually lost the fish and that it's got back into the wreck. But don't give up – a really big eel does feel like a doomed, sunken boat. Suddenly, you'll feel it come off the bottom and your heart, as well as the fish, will begin to lift. Now the battle begins in earnest. You'll need a butt pad, strength and plenty of determination. Eels can swim backwards, and this gives them an added trick up their sleeves. Once you have an eel off the bottom, make sure it doesn't get back there, and keep pumping. Lift the rod as high and as gently as you can, and then wind in furiously as you lower it again towards the sea's surface. Keep repeating this process and, little by little, the giant will come towards the sunlight.

Happily, in these more enlightened days, conservation is the key word. Gone are the days when dead and discoloured conger would litter the quays of Brixham and Plymouth. Ninety-nine per cent of fish, whenever humanly possible, are now returned alive to fight another day. The key is to bring the conger, as quietly as possible, to the boat side. A pair of long-handled pliers are clamped to the hook shank and then twisted until the hook comes free. Carry out the operation as carefully as you can.

For real, full-blooded, absolute power there's hardly anything in the sea to beat a big brute of a conger. It's an experience that every sea angler should go through. But, be warned, it can become addictive!

best for the tope. Squid also works well, as do cocktails of ragworm and squid. Try jellyworms, too, especially for pollack when the tide is easing. That is the real beauty of fishing in Bude Bay – you can run through a whole range of baits and methods and pick up anything from black bream to really serious tope.

Boscastle is a great venue once you're back on shore – cafés, restaurants and good pubs with plentiful accommodation. The National Trust actually owns the area and that means that it is always maintained in tiptop condition. Have fun!

⊨ ACCOMMODATION – phone the Boscastle Information Centre for all your accommodation requirements on 01840 250010.

○ TACKLE SHOPS – try Bude Angling Supplies, 6 Queen St, Bude on 01288 353396.

⇒ BOAT HIRE – a highly recommended skipper is Ken Cave, boss of the *Peganina*. He can be contacted on 01288 353565. Fred Siford is the Harbour Master at Boscastle and can arrange launching for your own boat; phone him on 01840 250453.

LYNMOUTH

Lynmouth is a typical north Devon coastal town – very picturesque, perfect for a holiday and with all manner of attractions for the family. It has good harbour possibilities and some cracking summer mackerel fishing. Trips run from the harbour in the centre of the town and are very scenic. Mind you, most times I've been out, I've been shown up badly... most recently being out-fished by a rather loud-mouthed American girl aged no more than six!

The harbour arm can be prolific at times, with tremendous possibilities for both bass and grey mullet – typical of the north Cornwall and Devon coast in fact. This is where the freshwater fisherman on holiday can really win out – simply pack your standard float and spinning gear and you can get some tremendous sport. Do, however, remember to rinse off any salt after the trip or you'll have problems with rust once you get home and autumn draws on.

And can I make a suggestion here? If you're in the area and you have either freshwater tackle with you or reasonably light sea gear, then make enquiries at the Tourist Centre as to whether there are any salmon up the East Lyn River.

Salmon generally run late in the summer but any high water can push them up much earlier than that. Indeed, anything can have an effect. For example, back in 2001, some porpoises came into the bay and began hunting the salmon that had gathered there preparing to run the river later in the year. Rather than face the onslaught from the porpoises, though, the fish began to run much earlier, following each and every tide over a couple of days or so. The result was that the river, for at least two to two and a half miles, was full of salmon between four and perhaps ten pounds – quite brilliant sport.

Get your day or week ticket from the Tourist Information Centre and make sure you have your Environment Agency freshwater licence to boot. The rest is up to you. I would advise getting a good supply of lobworm, a bait that is allowed on the river at certain times – check your ticket for up-to-date information. If you have fly gear with you, so be it, but I realise this is unlikely to be the case if you're a hard and fast sea angler!

Travel light – this is important. You want to seek out as many of the pools as you possibly can from the town right up into the moor.

Wear Polaroid glasses. This is essential so that you can watch the water in front of you – especially when the water is clear. With any luck at all, you should be able to see salmon moving in and out of the shallows and deeper runs.

Let's say you get to a pool and you can see a couple of salmon on the fin, perhaps in mid-water – you're in with a real chance. First of all, don't scare the fish. They will be very wary. Remember they have just come in from the sea, so they are constantly on the lookout for predators. Make use of every bit of cover that's available while you try to get close to the fish.

Two or three lobworms on a size six hook should suffice as bait. The big question is how much weight you're going to need. Use too much and the splash may well scare the fish. Also, you want to try and present the worms at the level they're swimming, so it pays to start light. Perhaps one or two SSG shot are all you're going to need. Try to work out the strength of the current and consider carefully where you are going to cast your bait. I'd advise putting it in two or three yards upstream of the fish so it gives them plenty of time to see it as it closes towards them. Remember, if you use a reasonably light line, your casting distance and accuracy will be greatly increased. I'd recommend something between eight and ten pounds.

Your worms are drifting towards the salmon. A fish of about seven pounds suddenly moves purposefully through the current and seizes it. You have a decision to make… delay the strike, as old-fashioned salmon anglers used to do, and you'll end up with a deep-hooked fish that will almost certainly have to be killed. Strike almost immediately and the fish will either get off or it will be hooked in the lip so that you can return it. The decision is, to some degree, yours and the ticket says that some fish may be retained for the table. However, can I make a plea with you and beg that the fish are returned. I know it's asking a lot, and a bright fresh-run salmon is a mouth-watering prospect, but do think about the good of the river in the future and the all-important question of the angler's image. Let's say it is summer. Let's say that the weather is decent. If it is, then there will inevitably be a whole procession of tourists walking along the riverside path up to the Watersmeet Centre. If these tourists see a fisherman bashing a fresh silver salmon to death with the nearest rock then, once again, the popularity of our sport takes a nose-dive. If, on the other hand, they see the angler keep the fish in the water, gently unhook it and watch it swim away, then our reputation is enhanced.

Perhaps salmon fishing isn't true sea fishing, but you are talking about a fish that spends the majority of its life in the sea. Moreover, you've got the sound and smell of the sea in your nostrils when you're fishing this lower stretch of river. Above all, this is an intriguing way to spend a day and that should be all that matters. In my book, it doesn't really matter whether you're going for big-beach midwinter cod, wrasse from a rock pool, tench from an estate lake or pike from a Scottish loch… it's the fact that we're all fishing that matters!

One piece of advice. If you can get out on the river with your ticket either very early or late – before or after the tourists have descended that is – you'll probably find that your chances are greatly enhanced.

If you do hook a fish, try to keep it in the pool. If you let it get out through the tail, then you'll be involved in a long scramble down perilous, rocky ground, which could prove bad for the fish and is potentially dangerous for you! Playing a fish hard is by far the best method on rivers such as this.

Don't be in too much of a hurry to leave behind the pools in the towns themselves. These frequently hold fish that are just in from the sea and these are often quite willing to make an open mouth at a passing worm.

Do take care of your lobworms, especially on a warm summer's day, because you'll find they're every bit as vulnerable to high temperatures as lugs and rags. Keep them in a damp tub, perhaps under moist newspaper or moss. Don't go too small on bait. Two, three, four or even five big lobs are what a salmon is looking for. But ring the changes. If you don't get any reaction with a big bait, then it doesn't do any harm to give it a cast or two with a small one.

ACCOMMODATION – for accommodation try the Exmoor National Park Visitor Centre on 01598 752509 – they are extremely helpful.

TACKLE SHOPS – sadly, I have to report that tackle is pretty well impossible to buy in either Lynmouth or Lynton – a good business opportunity for someone perhaps?

BOAT HIRE – for fishing trips, contact Matthew Oxenham on 01598 753207.

FLY RODDING IN THE SOUTH WEST

Fly rodding around the Devon and Cornish coastlines has been long established. Men such as Robin Armstrong and Ewan Clarkson helped pioneer the method decades ago. Today, experts such as Russ Symonds are taking the technique ever further.

First of all, what sort of species are really obtainable or pursuable on the fly? Well, certainly mackerel and, most glamorously, bass. You can also pick up mullet when they're really in a frenzy, packed together and feeding hard. Other fish will take a fly – notably pollack – but it's these three species that attract the bulk of fly-rodding attention.

And the tackle? Some of the guys use straightforward bonefish outfits. These, after all, are absolutely designed for the job and perfect for working through a light surf. Don't despair, though, if you've only got typical freshwater fly-fishing tackle. A floating line is probably what you're going to need and a general seven or eight weight outfit.

Flies? We're really talking lure fishing here... it's not dry fly fishing a chalk stream or nymphing for grayling! The generic term for what the bass and so on are feeding on is elvers – perhaps small eels, but just as commonly tiny fish of all species that tend to migrate together through the summer months. Therefore, you're using a fly that looks like anything small, silvery and edible. You can take it a bit further – one of the peak ways of taking bonefish in the warmer seas is on an imitation crab; these work brilliantly for bass.

Whereabouts? All these fish will come in very close indeed, and it's very much a stop, search and find type of method. Keep your eyes open – this is vital. On many occasions you'll see the ocean actually boiling as mackerel or bass are hammering into the prey shoals. Keep on the move. Keep your eyes open. Have binoculars with you and you'll see a whole sight more. You can pick all these species up off rocks, off the beaches, up estuaries – really anywhere that fish are coming in to forage.

The best times? Well, you don't want a big wind. This makes fly fishing difficult physically, and you don't want to run the risk of getting tangled up or, worse, doing yourself injury. Furthermore, a big wind can stir up the sand and make the water cloudy. Much better are temperate conditions – not too much wind and a reasonably clear sea. Obviously, if you can get out early or stay out late, then you are probably going to do best. In many places, it doesn't depend too much on the state of the tide. Even in low water, for example when fish get caught up estuaries, they will swim around not doing much in particular but willing to make a mouth at a tasty-looking fly.

And the technique? Remember that you don't have to strain massively to reach huge distances. Very often you will pick up bass just a few yards out actually in the surf. It's better to cast short distances and approach gently rather than splash around and scare the fish. You don't really need to work the fly much at all in a strong tide, the sea will do it for you. If, however, there's little flow – say you're up a low-water estuary – then it pays to give the fly some good old tweaks and keep it on the move, simulating a fleeing fish.

Whatever species you're after – mackerel and bass especially – expect a good, solid thump. They don't mess about when they're hitting into a prey fish and it's just the same when they're after your fly.

Of course, fly rodding doesn't necessarily mean that you're going to catch the most or the biggest bass, but what the heck? Believe me, a three- or four-pound school fish fights stupendously on fly kit and I'd rather catch half a dozen like that than fifty on feathers. And don't overlook the mackerel… in fact, a one-and-a-half-pound mackerel fights at least as well as a four-pound bass and that's saying a lot. The mullet, too, are something special on a fly rod. Oh, and one more thing if you're after mullet: don't overlook a very sparsely dressed nymph pattern – perhaps with a gold head bead to give a bit of weight and a bit of flash. Expect takes from mullet to be just a little less vigorous than those you pick up from bass or mackerel.

Above all, this is very much a pioneering method from which you can take some satisfaction. If you have a fly rod and you are heading for the south west, pack it. Ask the locals for advice – they're almost certain to prove helpful. Keep your eyes open and if you see surface feeding activity, get that rod out and you'll soon hear that reel screaming.

SEA-FISHING SITES IN WALES

Foreshore

Sand bank

100m

50m

50m

30m

30m

50m

ISLE OF ANGLESEY

Carmel Head • Amlwch

Holyhead   Anglesey

Holy Island

Great Ormes Head   Prestatyn

Llandudno   Colwyn   Rhyl

Conwy   Bay

River Dee

A5   Menai
Bridge
Llanfair Pwllgwyngyll   Bangor   Bethesda   CONWY   Flint

Menai Straits   • Caernarfon   River Conwy   FLINTSHIRE   Denbigh   Mold

Caernarfon Bay   Betws-
y-coed   DENBIGHSHIRE   Ruthin

Trefor   Porthmadog   Ffestiniog   Llangollen   Wrexham
WREXHAM

Lleyn Peninsula   Morfa Bychan   Bala

Pwllheli   Blackrock Sands

Abersoch   Tremadog   GWYNEDD
Bay

Barmouth   • Dolgellau
Mallwyd

ENGLAND

Welshpool

Cardigan Bay   Aberdyfi   • Machynlleth
Aberdovey Bar

Newtown

Aberystwyth

Llangurig

Rhayader   Knighton

Aberaeron

CEREDIGION   Lampeter   Builth Wells

Strumble Head   Cardigan   Newcastle
Emlyn   POWYS   Hay-on-Wye

St David's Head   Fishguard

St David's   PEMBROKESHIRE   CARMARTHENSHIRE   Brecon

Ramsey Island

St Brides   Narberth   Carmarthen   Llandeilo   Brecon
Bay   Haverfordwest   Beacons

Skomer Island   Wiseman's Bridge   St Clears   River Loughor   Ammanford   Abergavenny
Amroth   Marros   Merthyr   MONMOUTHSHIRE
Skokholm Island   Millford   Neyland   Pendine Beach   Llanelli   Tydfil   Pontypool
Haven   Saundersfoot Beach   Gowerton   Aberdare
Pembroke   Tenby   Carmarthen Bay   Pencleddau   Gorseinon   Mountain Ash   Cwmbran
Caldey Island   Swansea   Neath   CAERPHILLY
St Govan's Head   SWANSEA   Port   Pontypridd   Caerphilly   Newport
The Gower   Talbot   BRIDGEND   CARDIFF   NEWPORT
Worms   Mumbles   Bridgend   CARDIFF
Head   Mumbles   Pier   Porthcawl   Cowbridge
Head   Monknash   Barry   Sully Island
Summerhouse Point   Aberthaw
VALE OF GLAMORGAN

Bristol Channel

N

*Although I came to Wales for the quality of the freshwater
fishing, it wasn't long before I realised the outstanding sea
fishing available in the principality. Personally, I tend to be
quite selective about what I do when it comes to my
saltwater outings and Wales really offers some tremendous
treats. The bass fishing is superb and there are some very
interesting mullet possibilities. The sea trout are virtually
everywhere and the tope fishing can be fantastic. And if it's
cod you fancy, there's plenty of good sport around Newport,
Cardiff and Swansea. Try Fishguard, Conwy and the Menai
Straits too. One of the best things, from my point of view, is
that if you get out of the towns, just a little way, you'll find
plenty of deserted beaches and headlands. I'm used to
solitude when it comes to my freshwater fishing and, believe
me, with the huge expanse of coastline that Wales has to
offer, solitude is one thing you can easily find.*

PETER SMITH, HOTELIER AND WRITER

The coastline of Wales really does offer another world of
sea fishing. Some of it is stunningly beautiful and much
of it very remote. You really can get away from the madding
crowds in many parts of the principality. Ask local advice to
give you a starting point, but then strike out on your own
and do a bit of exploring. Wales is another prime holiday area
and it's possible to please both the family and the fisherman
in many locations. Moreover, after the foot and mouth
epidemic of 2001, the tourist industry everywhere is eager to
welcome people back into the countryside, and what could be
better than going there with a sea rod to hand. Peter makes a
point about the sea-trout fishing in Wales – well, it's virtually
the capital of sea-trout fishing in the UK, and, if you get the
chance, watch the Welsh boys at work. Believe me, they are
wizards and their skills might even inspire you to do a little
night fly fishing yourself.

NEWPORT

The south coast of Wales has long been a mecca for sea angling. Newport has a lot to offer, situated as it is at the throat of the Bristol Channel. A pal of mine has his own boat there that he launches to fish this area and, in the summer, he takes a bewildering number of species. He tells me the skate and ray fishing are unexpectedly good.

⊨ ACCOMMODATION – for details of accommodation in the area, contact the Tourist Information Centre in Newport on 01633 842962.

○ TACKLE SHOPS – phone Dave Richard's Angling Shop on 01633 254910 or the Pill Angling Centre on 01633 267211 for advice on fishing in the area.

CARDIFF

Cardiff has a lot going for it, too. Perhaps the first place to mention is the beach fishing at West Aberthaw, which you will find by heading towards Cardiff airport and continuing west along the B4265. Find the petrol station in Aberthaw itself and turn left down to a large car-park on the west side of the power station. You'll find the hot water outfalls to your left. The renowned Summerhouse Point is the rock headland on the right. This is a large bay – very rocky and weedy – so it's a real tackle-grabber. The cod fishing, especially in the winter, is something pretty special. It fishes best, the locals say, a couple of hours either side of low water. It looks good at high water, but results plummet quickly. As the ground is so rough, visit at low water to get some idea of the terrain. As a tip, try to fish from the highest ground you can find into deep water close in.

Favourite baits include lug, razor fish, squid and fresh peeler crab. As you can guess, this venue is very exposed to strong southerlies, so avoid these if there's a big swell on. Be very careful about establishing your exit route, particularly at night. If in doubt, ask the advice of locals.

We've concentrated on the cod, which are a really magnificent winter bonus, but there are other species on offer too. During the winter, you will come across pouting and whiting and there are some big conger about in the autumn and early part of the winter. In the summer, expect a lot of smooth-hound and bass, along with a few wrasse and, I'm told, even the odd trigger fish. And, once again, this is a perfect venue for my personal favourite style of sea fishing… using freshwater gear and a float for the plentiful mullet that love to feed amongst the weed and rocks. A great place all round.

It would be quite wrong to leave the Cardiff area without some mention of Sully Island, which is directly south of the city. For winter cod, this is a mark that's hard to beat. It's a small tidal island and you'll find it at the eastern end of Sully Bay. It's accessible for around two hours either side of low water. But do, do, do be warned – don't cross the tidal causeway connecting the island to the mainland, even if you think it's safe to do so. If you're in any doubt, ask the locals or enquire at the nearest tackle dealers.

Come winter, there are plenty of codling about, but it's the double-figure cod that really prove the attraction. Low water generally produces most of the cod, and top marks are Monkey Pole, a post on the island's eastern end, where forty- or fifty-yard casts are all you need out onto clean ground where the big cod feed. Green Island, to the south of Sully, offers rough ground but plenty of big cod as well. Top baits for the island include lug tipped with squid, ragworm and peeler crab. Look out for a gentle south-westerly, but as this is a very exposed area, too much wind can bring its own problems.

ACCOMMODATION – contact the Tourist Board in Cardiff on 029 2022 7281.

TACKLE SHOPS – contact Aspinall's Angling Supplies on 01446 742645 or Barry Angling Centre on 01446 747638.

MONKNASH

There are all manner of lanes leading to the sea from the B4265 road that runs westward from Barry. However, one of the favourite locations is at Monknash, a tiny little village beyond Llantwit Major that is very easy to miss. Get yourself to the pub, The Plough and Harrow, and turn down the lane for about half a mile towards the sea. Soon the road turns right and becomes a rough single-track. Park here and walk. Take the left fork, across the stile and through a wood. Allow twenty minutes for the walk. You'll find yourself on a wonderful beach that offers superlative ray fishing, probably the best in the area.

Thornbacks arrive as early as March, but the sport really heats up from mid-April right through to the autumn. Small-eyed ray abound and there are some good double-figure fish. There's some rough ground about, which attracts bass, conger and codling, but if you head for the large sandy area on your right and walk a good way into it, you should be able to fish over a clean bottom. This is very much a place to fish on the low tide. Approach it two or three hours down and the same up. Sand eel is rated by the locals as a top bait here. You'll find most of the bigger fish are pregnant females, so it makes sense for all future sport to put back the rays that you catch.

ACCOMMODATION – contact the Tourist Board in Bridgend on 01656 664906.

TACKLE SHOPS – there are two excellent contacts in the area – Ewenny Angling Supplies in Bridgend on 01656 662691 and the Barry Angling Centre in Barry on 01446 747638.

HOTSPOT – PENCLAWDD

I'm always looking out for intimate sea-fishing adventures, and there are few better places than Penclawdd, west of Swansea on the north Gower coast. Here, where the Loughor estuary meets the sea, you will find some close-in flounder-fishing of the highest quality. Penclawdd is probably at its peak from September right through to December, though you may well catch the bigger specimens in the early spring. The summer months here can also be really interesting, with some tremendous mullet and bass fishing.

It can be a bit of a hike through the marshes and mud, so waders, perhaps even chest waders, are advisable. Nonetheless, the scramble is well worthwhile. Indeed, the fish come so close in that some locals are even beginning to catch them on a freshwater pole set-up. You can, of course, leger for the fish – mullet, bass or flounder – with traditional gear, but they will come so close in that float fishing is always a really good option. A simple freshwater float rod can offer tremendous possibilities in these conditions.

The area does fish well, as you'd expect, on the flood tide. Neap tides are the ones to go for – the problem with the high tides is that they will fill up the dykes behind you and even come over the marsh itself. So, do be very careful and make sure that you check out the state of the water before you set out.

Harbour ragworm appear to be one of the top baits here – put a good few on the hook so that you've got an obvious, unmissable bait.

This really is an area that offers a great deal. You can often catch fish as close as twenty yards or less. Consider fishing light, so you can keep your bait on the move, and take seriously the idea of using freshwater float-fishing gear – you'll enjoy your sport even more. Imagine a good bass or mullet in such a situation...

Enjoy your surroundings, too – this is a pretty, wide-open place, which is a joy to fish, particularly when the sun is out and there's a light breeze on the in-coming tide.

You find it by following the M4 to junction 47 and exit at the signs for Gower. Make your way to Gowerton and then head west on the B4295 until you reach Penclawdd. If you just drive out of the village towards the west, you'll find the car-park. From here, you can walk to the channel. I repeat, it is a bit of a slog, so travel light and make sure that your footwear is up to the job.

The freedom of the high seas is a tremendous asset, especially during the summer when you can cruise looking for sandbanks or reefs – possible hotspots for bass or skate.

It pays to have a real armoury of leads, both in terms of shape and size. You'd be surprised how often one type of lead will grip bottom where all the others seem to fail.

The tide is on its way in among the Scottish Isles. This is the moment to look out for bass or sea trout, and even mullet can be found as far north as this.

Low water is definitely the time to do your detective work if you're thinking of bass fishing once the tide is in. Look for channels, gulleys and any other food-holding area.

An aerial view of the Scottish Isles shows the indented coastline that is so attractive to all species of fish and provides somewhere to cast a line whatever the weather.

Sea pools created by the ebbing tide are well worth looking at. Sea trout, bass, flatfish, mullet, and perhaps even wrasse, may well be willing to feed as they await the flow.

The tub gurnard is the largest of the gurnard family, sometimes exceeding two feet in length. Its long, strong rays allow the gurnard to forage in the mud for food.

SWANSEA

Moving westwards we come to Swansea, the city by the sea, set in a lovely bay midway along the coast. It's a busy port and has the second highest tidal range in the world! These facts alone give a lot of scope for the angler. One of the top shore marks is the East Pier and breakwater. To get there, follow the A483 from junction 42 on the M4 and motor on to Swansea Docks. Look out for the Queen's Dock and the breakwater. The Associated British Ports (ABP) allow anglers to fish the weirs but you must get a permit beforehand. Apply to the Port Manager, Harbour Office, Lockhead, Kings Dock, Swansea, SA1 1QR. The permit costs just over £20. There are some really good cod and whiting fishing, especially in the winter. Summer catches are generally made up of ray, smooth-hound, conger and bass.

If you continue along the A483, you will eventually come to the West Pier. This long pier offers some tremendous fishing and is very popular with the locals. The summer produces bass, mullet, dogfish and flounder, along with some plaice. Expect whiting and codling during the autumn and winter. It's a good place to float fish for mackerel in the summer and, if your gear is fine enough, you'll probably pick up a mullet or two on a small rag or even a pinch of breadflake.

The beach offers great opportunities and you can follow it westwards along the A4067, the Oystermouth Road. Eventually, you will reach the town of Mumbles. There are many access points and you'll find predominantly sand and mud as you approach the west. There's some rougher ground with some deep gullies. Expect to catch good bass, flounder, dab and dogfish through the summer. Winter again provides cod and whiting.

It's worth talking about Mumbles Pier. Some angling is permitted at a charge of £3 per rod but you must be off around dusk. The fishing is extraordinarily good and you will generally find plenty of space. Double-figure cod often show up in the winter and in the summer expect all the usual species with some tremendous bass fishing. Take a drop net with you – a double-figure bass is always on the cards.

From the pier, you can see the famous Mumbles Head and its lighthouse. This is a tidal island, noted for great bass fishing. The ground there is very rough, and do take care not to get cut off by an incoming tide. The Head is accessible for a couple of hours either side of low tide. The gullies between the islands are very productive and you'll find the current goes through at a fair lick. Try spinning in the summer and float-fished live prawn.

Before leaving the Swansea area altogether, we ought to look at an area popular with the locals – the River Loughor, situated just east of Llanelli. To get there, leave the M4 at junction 47 and head through the town of Gorseinon. You will see the river quite soon and access is possible at several places near railway and road bridges. This is a good spot for a visiting angler, especially one who likes a bit of light line-fishing and hasn't got too much time to spend. It's regarded as one of the top flounder rivers in the area, especially in the early months of the year. Mind you, it's also good in the summer for silver eels, mullet and bass. In fact, the mullet-fishing on light gear can be exceptional. For the flatfish, a standard flowing trace is generally used but many of the locals add beads to the hook bait as an added attractor. Start at low water and fish right the way up. Watch for the mullet coming in very close, feeding hard in shallow water. Put down some bread-mash ground bait and you will stand some chance of holding them.

⊨ ACCOMMODATION – phone the Swansea Tourist Information Centre on 01792 468321 or the Mumbles Tourist Information Centre on 01792 361302. The latter is particularly good on accommodation for the Gower Peninsula.

○ TACKLE SHOPS – for local advice, contact Roger's Tackle on 01792 469999, Mainwarings on 01792 202245, Hook, Line and Sinker on 01792 701190, Baits and Bites on 01792 480490 or Country Angling in Gowerton on 01792 875050.

⬅ BOAT HIRE – try *Blue Thunder Mark* on 01403 797974, *Lady Gail* on 08850 718572, *Susan Jane* on 01792 648033, *Sarah Louise* on 01792 798180 or the *Enterprise* on 01443 450602.

CARMARTHEN BAY AND PEMBROKESHIRE

Moving further west, we come to Carmarthen Bay – a succession of wild beaches that are paradise for the bass and flounder fishermen. These golden beaches include the well-known Pendine and Saundersfoot beaches. A little-known area is Amroth, a picturesque, small coastal village lying between Llanteg and Wiseman's Bridge. The beach faces south east and lies behind some high cliffs, so it's well sheltered from severe westerlies. You'll catch flounders, whiting, dogfish and rockling throughout the winter, with occasional bass showing up in mild conditions. There are lots of bass and flounder in the spring. In the summer, mackerel and dab show up. Ragworm is the top bait, along with razor fish and lugworm for the bass.

Amroth is a clean beach apart from a large area of rocks right in front of the village itself. These are visible at low water. The right-hand side of the beach offers deeper water. Fishing for bass is ideal after a good onshore surf, and you'll find night conditions particularly successful. Long-range casting isn't a big deal here and you rarely need to go further than eighty yards.

It's simple to get to Amroth: just follow the A40 west from Carmarthen to St Clears. Take the A477 signposted towards Tenby. Amroth is eventually signposted on the left. The Amroth Arms offers a welcoming haven after a windy and wet night session!

ⵒ **ACCOMMODATION** – for information on accommodation in the area, contact the Tourist Board in Carmarthen on 01267 221901 or the Tourist Board in Tenby on 01834 842402.

ⵔ **TACKLE SHOPS** – depending on where in the bay you find yourself, contact the following: Morris Bros Ltd, Troy House, St Julian St, Tenby on 01834 844789; Bay Fishing Tackle, High St, Saundersfoot on 01834 813115; The Fishfinder, 51 King St, Carmarthen on 01267 220226; Anglers Corner, 80 Station Road, Llanelli on 01554 773981.

CARDIGAN BAY

The west coast offers legendary bass fishing. There is both excellent surf fishing and spinning from the many rocky headlands. As we move north, we come to Cardigan Bay. This is really top tope country – as is much of the Welsh coast. However, here on the west, Aberdyfi, Aberystwyth and Pwllheli offer some great opportunities. You'll find tope in shallower water, hence the attraction of Cardigan Bay. You can sometimes pick them up off the beach, but more often you're going to have to hire a boat.

Tackle will usually be a reasonably heavy uptide rod and a 7000-sized multiplier. If you're fishing a slack tide and the boat isn't crowded, then you can get away with heavy carp gear, but you've got to know what you are doing because you don't want the fight to go on overlong and the fish to become overstressed. Keep your rig simple. A running leger is the norm, with a six- to eight-foot trace of 200-pound mono, and a size 6/0 or 8/0 tied and crimped to the end. It's a straightforward rig, but you'll have to change it after catching a couple of fish. Don't use stainless steel hooks, in case you have to leave a hook in a fish – you will want it to rust away and drop out.

Best baits are live eels and mackerel, but squid and dab have also been used with success. Tope prefer fresh bait to stale – they're not scavengers. Think about rubby-dubby – fresh minced mackerel is good but so are older blood and guts. Try to be after your tope when there's a reasonable tide running – the moving water carries the smell of the bait to hunting fish. May to October is the prime period for this part of the coastline.

A typical bite will be a couple of bangs on the rod tip followed by a screaming run, so it's vital to have your reel set correctly. Don't clamp down the clutch too tight or all you will see of the rod is a fast-disappearing handle. Tope will immediately drop a bait if they feel too much resistance, so you've got to get the drag set just right. Once that run starts, give it a second or two, then tighten up and strike. It was once common practice to delay the strike, even until the second run. This, however, resulted in a lot of deep-hooked and dead fish. Today, tope should always be released. To do this successfully, you need a good quality disgorger to hand. If the fish is hooked deeply, the kindest thing to do is to cut the trace as near to the fish's mouth as possible.

LOOKING AFTER YOUR TACKLE

It's very tempting to come back from a trip, dump your tackle either in the back of a van or in a shed and forget all about it. Don't. The seawater is bound to do it harm, sometimes irreparably.

• *Always wipe down your rods with a damp cloth and pay special attention to the eyes. Make sure all salt spray is wiped off.*

• *Wipe down the reel seats especially carefully and, from time to time, use a little light oil on them.*

• *A good strong rod holdall is good for carrying your rods along the beach, but is especially important if you are transporting them. It's all too easy to snap off a tip or an eye.*

• *After a session, wash your reels gently under a tap for a couple of seconds. Then wipe dry with a soft cloth. Let the reel dry out totally before putting it back in its bag. Don't blast your reel with water and don't immerse it. A gentle drizzle is enough.*

• *Your waders – especially neoprenes – are expensive, so look after them. Don't allow them to fester crumpled in a corner. If they remain damp, cracks will begin to appear. Rather, hang them upside down from a hanger. This will allow air to circulate and for them to dry off naturally and keep their shape.*

• *Your lamps are also important, so spray them with fresh water and wipe off. Wash any dirt off the glass globe. If you've got a headlight with rechargeable batteries, top them up at once. If they become exhausted, batteries don't recharge successfully.*

• *Dry off your rigs, your leads and especially your hooks. Your hook is everything, so wash it off in fresh water to prevent rusting.*

• *It is also vital to pay close attention to the state of your line, especially if it's been subjected to harsh conditions or been used over rocky ground. If you're in any doubt about whether the line has been frayed or weakened, remove it and refill your spool.*

• *Look after your catch, too. If you can, gut and clean it on the beach or on the boat, or at the very least as soon as you get home. Don't leave this job – all you will end up doing is wasting the bounty of the sea.*

• *Always ensure that you dispose of unwanted tackle and litter in a responsible fashion. Don't, under any circumstances, just shove it all under a big boulder hoping that it will never see the light of day. Disposal of nylon line is particularly crucial – any left on the beach could mean the death of a seabird.*

84

⊨ Accommodation – contact the Tourist Board in Aberystwyth on 01970 612125.

○ Tackle shops – try Aberystwyth Fishing Tackle Shop on 01970 611200.

⇒ Boat hire – in Aberystwyth, contact the *Spindrift* skippered by Jean Roche on 01544 388492; in Aberdyfi, contact *Isle de Nord* skippered by Dave Saddler on 01970 828844.

BARMOUTH

Lying between a mountain range and the sea on the mouth of the River Mawddach is the beautiful old town of Barmouth. It is a good fishing area to concentrate on. The harbour provides really good fishing, especially for beginners. Walk along the breakwater and fish off the shingle bank back into the harbour. You will find the seabed is very clean, although the inside edge near to the breakwater is rougher.

You can get away with spinning rods and twelve-pound line, especially for the bass, flatfish and eels. A two-ounce weight should be quite enough. Long casting is not necessary and try to keep within the thirty- to fifty-yard mark. This is also a top area for mullet – try a tiny bar spoon tipped with ragworm. Light float-fishing with tiny strips of mackerel can also produce fish. You might also pick up garfish. Dab fishing is excellent from spring right through to autumn, when the whiting move in. Mullet and bass throng the area through the summer.

This is an easy spot to find: enter Barmouth on the A496 and take the Promenade Road. You will soon find the car-park on the beach front. Head for the boats at the eastern end of the car-park and pick up the footpath along the breakwater. Where the concrete breakwater starts and the sand dunes end, you will find a shingle beach. Fish facing the harbour.

⊨ Accommodation – contact the Tourist Board in Barmouth on 01341 280787.

○ Tackle shops – for up-to-the-minute advice contact the Seafarer Fishing Tackle Shop, Church Street, Barmouth on 01341 280978.

BLACKROCK SANDS AND PORTHMADOG

Carrying on further north, we come to a favourite mark called Blackrock Sands, near Porthmadog. To get there, find Woolworth's in Porthmadog itself and take the road signposted Morfa Bychan and Blackrock Sands. Take the road through Morfa Bychan until you come to the beach. This does get quite busy in summer, so early and late are best. Blackrock itself is the name given to the northern stretch of the beach. The name comes from the small rocky headland that dominates the fishing.

The beach itself doesn't have many features, so it pays to get close to the rocks themselves. Summer fishing is absolutely excellent for bass. They arrive some time in May and generally stay around until October or so. Also, in the summer you will come across dab and flounder. Early and late in the year, you find that some of the thornbacks move just within casting distance. A lot of the locals favour the mark in the autumn when huge numbers of whiting come in – these arrive during September, but thin out in December. During the summer, there are massive shoals of mackerel and garfish that come in close to feed on sprats and small fish – great for the kids in the family. This is great sport on very light spinning gear. Take one or two for the pan and you'll appreciate just how good they taste fresh from the sea.

⊨ ACCOMMODATION – contact the Tourist Board in Porthmadog on 01766 512981.
○ TACKLE SHOPS – contact the Fisherman, Central Buildings, High Street, Porthmadog on 01766 512464.

NORTH WALES

Next, we come to the small port of Trefor, on the north Welsh coast, just south of Anglesey. This really is a place best fished from your own boat, and launching is moderately charged at just over £6. The port used to be famous for smooth-hound, and the latest information is that these appealing fish are very much on the return. Look for them west of the harbour during the early part of the summer. They are generally found over sandy, clean ground. Peeler crabs are a great bait and pick up other species such as bull huss and thornbacks. Failing crab, try strips of mackerel or squid. To get the very best out of the fishing, don't go too heavy. In fact, stepped-up pike tackle is probably all you need. Go for a rod with, say, a three-pound test curve and load up with ten- or fifteen-pound line. This way, those smooth-hounds, with those great big pectoral fins of theirs, will really give a good account of themselves.

If you have a boat, you'll really like Trefor. The locals couldn't be more friendly and there's a really nice atmosphere to the place. There are plenty of fish around – especially now that most are being put back.

The north Welsh coast begins in earnest at Bangor, centre for the Menai Straits and Anglesey. This is a top area in very scenic conditions. Further east, the Conwy estuary is particularly good for flatfish. You'll also find bass and mullet running up in the summer months. Winter produces larger whiting and codling, although the rougher ground around Llandudno offers the best chance for codling and coalfish.

Still further to the east lies the attractive holiday resort of Rhyl. This offers a whole range of fishing year round. There's plenty of both shore and charter-boat opportunities available.

BAIT TIPS

Fish aren't ravenous all the time and on occasion they need to be encouraged, especially when your time is tight. Adding something to the bait in terms of visuals and flavour can sometimes do the necessary trick.

• It often pays to attach a spoon some six inches or so up the trace from your bait. This gives a visual signal as well as sending out vibrations. It could be that bigger fish think a small flatty is trying to make off with the bait.

• Putting beads on the trace above the hook has long been part of the sea-angling scene. The newer booby beads are especially good as the metallic rattle attracts fish. Use a combination of colours.

• It's important to catch your quarry's eye – try a strip of squid or mackerel, on or above the hook.

 • Cocktails can really work a miracle and stimulate a tired appetite. Mind you, just simply loading different baits onto a hook isn't necessarily the answer and it needs thought. Try lug and cockles, or rag and strips of mackerel belly. Peeler crab and sand eel strips work well, as do lug and pieces of squid.

• Pilchard oil really draws fish in. Apply it from a plastic squeezy bottle; it's expensive but worthwhile. Cod liver oil is cheaper and can work, while there are those that swear by WD40!

• Try putting a big swim feeder, such as coarse fishermen use, twelve inches or so up the trace. Pack this with a pilchard oil-soaked rag and/or bits of left-over bait.

• There is also a host of shop-bought additives that you can try. A lot of them work well on the fish.

• If you're float fishing, for example, close in off rocks or even from a boat, it can pay to ground bait the area. Make a mini rubby-dubby out of fish, worm or whatever, and feed it so that it falls slowly through the water. This is particularly attractive to wrasse and bass.

• There are times when fish want a bait presented to them in a different manner. Flounder, for example, will frequently take a bait that's fished above the bottom and on the move, whereas they will refuse one that's static and legered.

• If you're fishing the estuaries, try maggots bought from the local tackle shop. These can be especially effective for mullet and it's worth trying a big bunch for flatfish.

⊨ ACCOMMODATION – details of accommodation can be obtained from the Tourist Information Centres in Llandudno on 01492 876413 and Colwyn Bay on 01492 530478.

○ TACKLE SHOPS – contact Happy Valley Angling, Llandudno Pier, North Parade, Llandudno, on 01492 877678. In Colwyn Bay, contact Rhos-on-Sea Fishing on 01492 544829 and the Victoria Angling Centre, Victoria Pier, on 01492 530663.

⊨ BOAT HIRE – contact Bangor Angling Supplies on 01248 355518. In Rhyl, try Blue Shark Fishing Trips on 01745 350267.

ANGLESEY

Let's now have a look at the island of Anglesey, beginning at Holyhead on the north of the island. The big feature here is the Holyhead breakwater, well over a mile long and renowned for both summer and winter fishing. Inside the breakwater the fishing is easier as there are fewer snags, but it's outside, over rough ground, that the best of the sport is to be had. Sometimes you can drive your car along the breakwater, but at other times it is closed and you have to walk. There are good spots right along and it's useful to ask local advice. Take note of that rough ground: make your tackle simple and always with a rotten bottom in case you have to pull for a break. Top baits are lug, rag, crab and squid. Another problem with the breakwater, apart from the rough ground, is the high wall. You need a drop net and, ideally, a good mate. Not a venue for juniors or elderly people.

In the summer, you can expect wrasse, dogfish, pollock; later on, smooth-hound, conger and ray. In the winter, look out for whiting, codling and coalfish. Boat fishing is also good – expect tope and thornback.

Moving clockwise round the island we come to Amlwch, which has a really good reputation for skate, conger and tope from the boats. There's also some good herring and mackerel fishing in the summer.

Beaumaris, on the south-east tip of the island, is renowned for boat fishing. From here, charter boats fish the Menai Strait, which is sheltered from prevailing south-westerly winds. Even if the winds are coming from the north or east, it is still possible to move down the Strait towards Caernarfon Bay. Caernarfon Bay is a real favourite – rays into double figures, tope to fifty pounds and big bull huss, along with mackerel and dogfish. There are also a few sandbanks that hold good numbers of bass and even the odd turbot.

⊨ ACCOMMODATION – contact the Tourist Information Centre at Llanfair PG on 01248 713177, or in Holyhead on 01407 762622.

○ TACKLE SHOPS – try the the Pilot Store and Fishing Tackle on 01407 831771.

⊨ BOAT HIRE – Stan Zalot runs Starida Sea Services, contact him on 01248 810250 for details of the extensive boat fishing available. Other contacts are Dave Jones, Beaumaris Marine Services on 01248 810746, and Anglesey Boat Company on 01248 810359.

LOOKING AFTER THE FISH

Fifty years ago, it was normal to slaughter everything caught either on the beach or from a boat. Today, this is no longer the case. Stocks of fish are much lower and have to be preserved. Also, we need to think about our image. Times have moved on and we need to be much more considerate, caring and conservation-minded, for our own good as well as for the good of the sea.

• *Only ever take home fish that you plan to eat. Underestimate, rather than overestimate, your needs.*

• *Naturally, return all under-sized fish at once.*

• *If at all possible, hold your fish in the water until they are strong enough to swim off, and don't allow them to drift away with the tide.*

• *Don't drop fish off piers or high-sided boats.*

• *Weigh fish (if you must) in slings and not from the gill.*

• *Keep shark species in the water. If you take them out, then without the buoyancy of the water to keep them in shape, their guts will drop under their own weight; this can easily lead to the rupturing of small blood vessels. Also, remember that all big fish thrash around on a boat or on the beach and can do themselves harm.*

• *Chat to your boat skipper before booking him up and ask him to return any fish that aren't required or which are inedible; conger are one of the best examples.*

• *It's the same with bait – don't dig or take more than you're going to need. Try to preserve any left over carefully for your next trip.*

• *When bass fishing from the shore, try not to take the fish from the water at all. You can simply play the fish out, lead it into the shallows and there slip the hook free with a pair of forceps. It's taking the fish out of its own environment that does the most harm.*

• *To avoid deep-hooking fish, strike as soon as is practical and avoid giving a fish the time to swallow the bait down deep.*

• *If you do hook a fish down deep that is bleeding from the gills, you are advised to kill it immediately. Once the fish is losing any amount of blood in that way, its chances of survival are minimal.*

Sea-fishing Sites in North-West England

SCOTLAND

ENGLAND

DUMFRIES AND GALLOWAY

Moffat
Langholm
Lockerbie
Dumfries
Longtown
Newton Stewart
Brampton
Stranraer
Bowness-on-Solway
Carlisle
Skinburness
Silloth
Kirkcudbright
Solway Firth
Luce Bay
Allonby
Maryport
CUMBRIA
Penrith
Appleby-in-Westmoreland
Workington
Brough
Whitehaven
St Bees
Ambleside
ISLE OF MAN
Point of Ayr
Andreas
Ramsey
Maughold Head
Ballaugh
Ravenglass
River Esk
Lake District
Windermere
Kendal
Peel
Laxey
St John's
Foxdale
Douglas
Douglas Head
Ulverston
Arnside
Kirkby Lonsdale
Port St Mary
Castletown
Barrow-in-Furness
Morecambe
Calf of Man
Dreswick Point
Isle of Walney
Lancaster
IRISH SEA
Fleetwood
LANCASHIRE
Blackpool
Burnley
Preston
Blackburn
Southport
Rochdale
Bolton
New Brighton
Wallasey
MANCHESTER
Hilbre Island
LIVERPOOL
Birkenhead
Otterspool
Warrington
Knutsford
MERSEYSIDE
River Mersey
Runcorn
Ellesmere Port
Macclesfield
Chester
Congleton
CHESHIRE

100m
200m
30m
50m
100m
50m
30m

M6
A74
A75
A596
A66
A591
A685
A683
A590
A59
M61
M58
M62
M56

N

Foreshore
Sand bank

The Lake District is much underrated when it comes to sea fishing. There's very little commercial activity, and the whole area is pretty well unexploited. For many years, I had a boat based in Ravenglass and the tope fishing was excellent. Very often I'd get anything up to a dozen fish in a day, including some big ones. The best I caught was fifty-seven pounds but I actually saw a monster of seventy-four pounds. There's also good pollack fishing, cod to double figures and great spur dog. The skippers in Whitehouse and Workington have located wrecks and you can also get out of St Bees. If you go twenty miles, you'll come across more wrecks, which give up pollack, cod and ling. I haven't even mentioned the bass fishing in the Esk estuary. There are some big mussel beds and some big fish come in. The Ravenglass estuary is also very good. Look for the rocks and punch a bait out. There really are some hot possibilities.

ANDY NICHOLSON, WRITER AND TV PRESENTER

My experiences off the coast of north-west England go back to 1961, a club outing out of Fleetwood into the storm-tossed waters of Morecambe Bay. I was initially put to shame by the beery anticipation of the adult members of the club who felt that a crate each was a prerequisite for the day. However, a short way out, my modest provisions of a flask and plain sandwiches began to look more sensible. Within half an hour of arriving at our chosen mark, I was the only one out of thirty people still with a rod in my hand. Sickness I'd obviously seen before that day, but never to this grotesque gothic level. The skipper maintained the torture for some three and a half hours, by which time the boat was beginning to look as though it had been struck by bubonic plague. The fact that I'd caught two dabs and an eel made me unpopular with the rest of the club members, but that I was capable of eating my lunch confirmed that I was to be loathed for the rest of that season.

MERSEYSIDE

Historically, the waters around Merseyside have been regarded as little more than open sewers. However, the Environmental Agency has put a lot of the wrongs of the past decades to right with brave and pioneering work. New sewage treatment plants have played a major part and now next to no crude sewage is being pumped into the river. In short, the Mersey estuary is now proving a revelation. Over thirty species of fish have been recorded, with coarse fish colonising the top of the water and more and more species pushing upwards. Even sea trout have been reported. There's talk, too, of salmon not being far off.

Dinghy fishing is possibly the best way to fish in the Mersey. Boats tend to go outside the river in the summer and stay inside during the winter. This isn't something forced upon them by the weather but more a trend induced by the habits of the fish. During the summer months, the river is good for plaice and flounder and you can expect the odd bass or two. Make sure that you have a chart, or, preferably, go out with a skipper or someone who knows the area. You really do need to head for the top marks. For example, Dukes Buoy is highly regarded as a cod area, whereas The Dee and Hilbre Island are good places for early summer tope. Jordan Spit can offer tope, rays, gurnards and some good mackerel fishing. There are plenty of shallow-water wrecks in the Mersey estuary and some of them produce conger. In winter, boats head well up-river and you'll see them dotted around the Liver Buildings and off Cammel Lairds, too.

Weather isn't too much of an issue as the Mersey is well-sheltered from the common south-westerly and westerly winds, but avoid north-westerlies or south-easterlies. You don't need to be far out, as most of the fish are close in to the edges. This is a help in strong winds and it does keep you out of the main shipping lanes. If you want to get out on the water and it's too far to bring your dinghy, charter boats are available to get you to the wrecks, although overfishing has depleted cod stocks in particular. Expect pollack and conger with the odd huss, spur dog, tope and ray.

There's a lot on offer for the shore fisherman. There are plenty of fish year round and well within casting range. You can expect fish from the river mouth as far up as Otterspool. The problem for the shore angler is that a lot of the river is made up of docks and steep walls that you just can't access. However, there is good beach fishing around New Brighton and it is possible to fish from some of the best dockside on the Liverpool side of the river. Alexandra Dock, Gladstone Dock and the Seaforth Rocks can be fished by permit holders. Permits are available from the North West Association of Sea Anglers on 0151 5260197. You will catch some cod and whiting in the winter, with flatfish, eels and some bass in the summer. In the winter, the river really does flow muddy, so fish hunt very much by scent rather than sight. For that reason it is very important to keep your bait freshened up – big, black lug is a favourite hereabouts.

⊢⊣ ACCOMMODATION – contact the Tourist Information Centre in Liverpool on 0906 680 6886.

○ TACKLE SHOPS – contact Star Angling on 01744 738605, The Tackle Shed on 01744 810805, Fisherman on 0151 6534070 or J. E. Robinson on 01744 534136.

⛵ BOAT HIRE – contact Liam McElroy on 0151 2807445.

FROZEN BAITS

Anglers don't always have the luxury of fresh baits, especially if they are travelling. For example, it's generally not possible to carry worms or crabs long distances in the car, especially in sunny weather. Also, you might well be visiting an area that is just too far from a top-quality tackle shop. And how about those impromptu sessions where you just fancy the odd quick cast? Well, frozen baits can help you out to some degree, especially if you've got the facility to move them from one freezer to the next.

• You'll probably need a cool box and ice packs. These will prolong the life of your bait considerably. Take bait from just one packet at a time to avoid waste.

• When you do open a packet of bait, cover it with a rag soaked in saltwater to prevent a fast thaw in the sun.

• Try to buy frozen baits from a big shop with a fast turnover. The bait is more likely to be fresh that way. Watch out for giveaway signs such as ice crystals in the bag – a sure sign of poor freezing or long past shelf date.

• Sprats are often better as bait when they are blast-frozen, as they're not so soft and can be cast a greater distance – especially if they're tied on with thread.

• Peeler crab are excellent frozen. Keep all the bits and pieces that fall off them to tip off your worm baits in the winter.

• Shellfish and calamari squid freeze well. Buy squid in bulk for economy. Put the frozen block in the microwave at thaw setting. Break away individual pieces for refreezing in trip-sized packs.

• When freezing at home, try to ensure the bait is as dry as possible. Kitchen tissue soaks up moisture well. Also try to ensure that all the air is forced out of the bag to avoid freezer burn or dehydration.

NEW BRIGHTON

Before leaving Merseyside completely, let's look at one very famous mark – Perch Rock Beach at New Brighton. The beach on the east side of the Perch Rock is very much a low-water venue. At high water, the currents are often too strong for reasonable fishing. This mark is a godsend for locals and visitors alike, as it does fish pretty much year round.

The spring sees some good flatfish – both flounder and plaice. The summer sees good numbers of small bass, with the occasional bigger one putting in an appearance. September and October really see things hotting up, with whiting and codling moving into the Mersey in increased numbers. You'll find them hanging on throughout the winter months and it's probably only February and March when the area is really in the doldrums. We're not talking big fish here. The whiting are probably not much more than a pound. You can expect codling of a couple of pounds or so, though the odd big fish does show up occasionally.

Crabs appear to be the most popular bait during the summer months for the school bass, whereas cocktails go down well for the codling. Try lug tipped with mackerel or mussel.

To get there from Liverpool, use the Kingsway Mersey tunnel and then look for signs for New Brighton. Get on to the King's Parade (the A554). You will see the Fort at Perch Rock before reaching New Brighton – turn off the main road towards it.

⊨ ACCOMMODATION – there is accommodation available but don't expect to find it on top of the fishing – this is an industrial rather than a tourist area. Phone the Tourist Information Centre in Liverpool on 0906 680 6886.

○ TACKLE SHOPS – there's a wealth of tackle shops in the area, all of which can give excellent, up-to-the-minute advice. Contact Ken Watson on 0151 6384505, Ken Hopkins on 0151 6778092, Winnicott Tackle on 0151 4282718, Anfield Tackle on 0151 2608223, Champs Tackle on 0151 4943029, Sharps Fishing Tackle on 0151 9282626, Johnson's Angling Centre on 0151 5255574 and Tasker's Angling Centre on 0151 2606015. Try also John's Bait and Tackle in Wallasey on 0151 6391069 or Parkes Angling in Birkenhead on 0151 6520606.

BLACKPOOL AND MORECAMBE

Blackpool and Morecambe remain two very popular holiday centres in the north west and although the fishing might not be of the highest quality, both areas offer quite enough to make it worth packing the tackle if you're off on holiday. Fleetwood, between the two, is where I began my fishing career, and it is also worth a visit. At Blackpool, there are seven miles of beach fishing available, as well as sport from the North Pier.

The problem is that Blackpool's beaches do get very busy in the hot summer periods. Early and late in the day offer the best opportunities. In fact, it is probably better to get afloat. At Morecambe there is plenty of beach and jetty fishing yielding flatfish, bass and eels during the summer months. Expect some codling and whiting in the winter. Heysham harbour and North Wall offer good opportunities for a wide range of species year round. You can pick up anything from conger to mullet during the summer.

⊨ ACCOMMODATION – contact the Tourist Information Centre in Blackpool on 01253 403223 or in Morecambe on 01524 582808.

○ TACKLE SHOPS – contact Morecambe Angling Centre on 01524 832332 and Charlton and Bagnall, 3–5 Damside Street, Lancaster on 01524 63043. In Fleetwood, contact Langhorne's on 01253 872653 for information and some good fresh bait.

◆ BOAT HIRE – contact P. Atkinson on 01253 825217 for charter possibilities. In Fleetwood, C. B. Bird offers charter hire on 01253 873494 or contact the *Viking Princess*, a favourite boat of the area, on 01253 873045.

ARNSIDE AND BARROW-IN-FURNESS

Moving into Cumbria, Arnside is a quaint little village situated on the south side of the River Kent estuary. The place is gaining a reputation as one of the best flounder marks in this part of the country. Throughout the year, the fish average a pound, but something three times this size is always possible, especially in the winter. You can fish the mark when the tide is out and the fish are concentrated into the channels that remain. You'll find these are deeper just seawards of the village's small pier. However, they're closer to the shore upstream near the viaduct. This means that casting is easier and you can get away with lighter gear. By and large, the bottom is comparatively snag-free, though you'll see the odd rock outcrop amongst the sand and mud.

Fish the mark a couple of hours either side of low water for the best results. But, be warned – there can be a strong tidal bore here and sometimes this can reach two feet in height and catch you out if you're unaware. Ask advice from the locals and, most importantly, if you hear the warning siren, gather up your belongings and move very quickly away from the bank. This is a top spot, but do take all precautions.

Tackle rather depends on where you are fishing. If you're going for one of the further channels, then you might need to cast anything up to eighty yards or so, which calls for standard beach tackle. If, however, you look for one of the closer in marks, lighter gear will do. The locals swear by harbour ragworm, and it can work even better with a piece of mackerel hooked up as a cocktail. Lugworm can also take fish. Don't go for small baits – flounders are greedy creatures and, in murky conditions, home in on a big, smelly bait.

The fishing is easy to find. Leave the M6 at junction 36, follow the A65 and turn off for Crooklands. Once in Crooklands, turn left onto the B5282 and this will take you into Arnside. Park near the viaduct.

Moving round to the west of Morecambe Bay, Barrow-in-Furness offers some good boat and shore fishing, especially for tope and bass in the summer months. Expect some codling and whiting in the winter.

⊨ **ACCOMMODATION** – contact the Tourist Information Centre in Barrow-in-Furness on 01229 894784.

○ **TACKLE SHOPS** – for further details on the sport in this region, contact Charlton and Bagnall in Lancaster on 01524 63043, Fawcett's (also in Lancaster) on 01524 32033, Gerry's of Morecambe on 01524 422146 and the Morecambe Angling Centre on 01524 823332.

⛵ **BOAT HIRE** – contact Stewart McCoy, skipper of the *Revenge*, on 01229 826160.

WORKINGTON

Travelling north, Workington offers some good possibilities. The harbour, for example, is well worth looking at. Here, at the mouth of the River Derwent, there's some good sport, with eels, flounder, occasional plaice and bass throughout the summer months. As the year wears on, you begin to find whiting and codling. What's good about the area is that the channel itself is protected on all sides – to the south by the breakwater and to the north by a jetty. This means that you can fish here in comfort through most conditions, even high winds.

Another good thing about Workington is that the bottom is not too rough and you don't have to fish any great distance – certainly thirty to forty yards is quite sufficient for most occasions. This means that you can use light gear and really make the most of the generally small-sized fish on offer.

You'll find the sport here begins in the spring, with the eels and flatfish. The bass, if they're going to appear, will follow on soon afterwards. The codling and whiting fishing is at its best from October onwards. An onshore wind is particularly good, packing the codling, especially, into the estuary. The mark fishes at most stages of the tide. Finding the mark is easy – simply follow the A597 into Workington and keep to the south side of the river. You'll find plenty of parking along the harbour wall.

⊨ **ACCOMMODATION** – contact the Tourist Information Centre in Workington on 01900 606699.

○ **TACKLE SHOPS** – contact Graham's Gun and Tackle on 01900 605093.

HAVE YOU CAUGHT YOURSELF A RECORD?

It's the dream of every angler to catch a fish that will immortalise him or her with a place in the record books. Line class records are taken very seriously in the world of sea fishing, but what do you do if you think you've won the lottery and landed that whopper?

• *First of all, it's essential to fill in a claim form. This needs to be completed and sent off within sixty days of the capture of the fish.*

• *You will need a clear photograph of the catch, so there's no doubt as to its identity. Also photograph any notable distinguishing marks.*

• *Keep a long sample of the reel line that you were using when you caught the fish.*

• *Get a scale certificate to say that the scales upon which the fish was weighed have been checked by an independent assessor.*

• *The claim will be acknowledged and you will be told what records you are being considered for.*

• *All information can be obtained from David Wood, The Light Tackle Club, 78 Beech Road, Horsham, West Sussex, RH12 4TX. Phone him on 01403 217884.*

• *If accepted, you will get a certificate, a badge and your place in the record books! But remember, fame isn't everything. Only put a fish through the stress of being weighed if you're sure you've got a whopper.*

MARYPORT

Just a few miles further north in Cumbria, Maryport is building up a good reputation for sea fishing. The port boasts a flourishing fishing fleet, along with a maritime museum and, of special interest to anglers, the Lake District Coast Aquarium. If you want to see how your favourite species actually look in the water, this is the place to go to. It is easily accessed via the A66 and A594 from the M6.

There is good shore fishing, which makes it attractive to the casual visitor. The promenade, especially, offers easy access, but there are some very productive rocky outcrops to the south of the town. Look around here for Black Banks, a couple of miles from the centre. Access is close to Siddick village. Excellent fishing, but do be careful of the quickly rising tide. Both piers at the town are open to fishing and the best of the sport is about two hours each side of high tide. Forget low water.

Maryport is really the flatfish centre of the north west and you can expect some really good-sized plaice over the two-pound mark. Flounders are also of an impressive size. You'll also see some mullet and bass during the summer months. Codling and whiting begin to show up during the early winter. The best of the sport is generally after dark. All the usual baits work well – lug, white ragworm and peeler crab being local favourites. You can buy most baits locally or dig them yourself.

Before leaving Maryport, let's have a look at another local mark, Grasslot Beach. You'll find this south of the Harbour Arms in Maryport and it's very much a favourite amongst locals from the late summer onwards. In fact, September to December is the peak period when large numbers of codling in the two- to three-pound bracket move close inshore. You'll also pick up some whiting and perhaps even a few dogfish. Fish the beach on larger, flowing tides, especially at night. You'll find a south-westerly wind also pushes fish closer inshore. Whilst most of the locals favour the autumn and early winter, this is also a good place for the visitor during the summer, with large bags of plaice and flounder to be caught. Lugworm works well throughout the year and some of the larger flatfish also come to peeler crab.

Just north of Maryport, you will find Allonby, an area principally of mud and sand where you will catch plenty of flounder to two pounds and plaice up to four pounds. Halfway between Allonby and Silloth, you'll come to Dubmill Point, which again is excellent for flatfish but does involve a long walk at low tide. Do avoid the racing flood tide as you can get caught out. Watch what the locals are doing and retreat in safety.

⊨ ACCOMMODATION – phone the Tourist Information Centre in Maryport on 01900 813738.

○ TACKLE SHOPS – there's no tackle shop anymore in Maryport, the last one closing down a short while ago. However, contact Graham's Gun and Tackle in nearby Workington on 01900 605093 or the Tackle Shack in Whitehaven on 01946 693233. These shops will not only sell you all the tackle and bait you need but will advise on the numerous competitions held throughout the year.

⇒ BOAT HIRE – Peter Hewitt on 01900 817926 can arrange charter-boat hire from the town.

SILLOTH TO BOWNESS-ON-SOLWAY

Moving up the Solway Firth to the north-west tip of Cumbria, you come to the town of Silloth, very much a Victorian relic with its wide, cobbled streets and impressive promenade. From here you get awe-inspiring views across the Solway Firth towards the imposing Scottish Borders. This is a great area for the holidaying angler and his family. Nice scenery, pleasant and relaxing, with lots to do and plenty of accommodation.

In Silloth itself, Tommy Legs is very popular and you'll find it close to the entrance of the dock. There's some slightly deeper water here and

flounder and plaice are again the main species. There's the odd codling or
two as well, although not particularly big ones, and even an occasional
thornback. The promenade stretches eastward from the town and offers
hugely accessible fishing. Like Maryport, Silloth offers some amazingly
good flatfish possibilities during the summer months. This means you
won't need particularly heavy gear, although a standard beach caster will do
fine. Your main line can be around the ten- to fifteen-pound mark and bait
can either be bought or dug locally. Silloth is very much a shore-fishing
area, both east and west of the town. You'll find a good range of ground
from rocky scars to clean, sandy beaches. Access is easy as the road runs
alongside the coastline. Long hikes, therefore, aren't generally necessary.

Skinburness is just a little further up the coast, and offers shallow water
over a sandy beach. Flatfish are again numerous, but there are plenty of
school bass in the summer months. Not large fish, but they give great
sport at around a couple of pounds in weight.

Finally, try Bowness-on-Solway, the legendary end of Hadrian's Wall.
This is a top mark and you can often expect a really good bag of flatfish.
Most anglers fish just in front of the village, a real beauty spot. Remember
that anglers are very much on show here to the general public, so make it
a constant rule to tidy up not only your own rubbish but anything else
you might find in your vicinity. There are no charter boats available in the
area, but if you bring your own dinghy, you can launch it from the public
slipway at the lifeboat station situated on the promenade. Getting out that
little bit further is bound to give you a head start, but it's not essential.

ACCOMMODATION – for accommodation phone the Tourist Information Centre in Silloth
on 01697 331944.

TACKLE SHOPS – see the entry for Maryport for details of tackle shops in the area.

THE ISLE OF MAN

Perhaps the cream of all the fishing in the north west can be enjoyed on
the Isle of Man. The island, though small, offers huge variety. To the
north, you're looking at typical surf beaches. To the south, the coastline
is more rocky. Moreover, the Isle of Man is a great holiday destination
and once again you're looking at a place that can be enjoyed by the
whole family, as well as the angler. To some degree, the sea fishing on
the Isle of Man has not been largely exploited, and you'll do well to go
there expecting a certain amount of adventure.

Douglas offers a great deal – expect to catch flatfish, especially large
sole, pollack, dogfish, coleys, pouting and a few codling from both the

USING SQUID AS BAIT

Squid is a cracking bait and you should always try to have some with you. It's a staple foodstuff for virtually every fish, and can turn a blank day into a really hum-dinging one. It's relatively cheap and it's almost universally available from supermarkets, fishmongers or tackle shops.

• *Most anglers use a whole squid, especially for big fish such as cod, conger or tope. This will require a pennel rig – two hooks on the same hook snood. There are all manner of variations that you can use but one of the most common is to slide a 3/0 onto the trace line. You then tie on a 6/0 to the end. Put the point of the big hook through the squid's body so the point is buried inside. Push the rest of the hook inside the body. Using a pair of forceps, work the hook down through the squid and pull it out of the opening by the head. Now pass the point of that hook through the eyes. Pull the second hook down so that the point sits just above the end of the body. Wrap the trace line round the hook three times and simply pass the point through the tail of the squid. Take hold of the large hook and slowly pull the trace line above the second hook to tighten everything.*

• *For smaller species – especially sole – you'll need much smaller strips that have been cut from the main body of the squid. Cut off the head, then cut through one side of the body. Open the squid out, remove all the innards, and cut strips about three inches long and around half an inch wide. To hook up, simply put the hook through one end of these strips.*

• *For species such as rays, a half squid is a preferred compromise. Simply cut the squid in half and use either the head or the tail section.*

• *Strips of squid with rag and lugworm make excellent cocktails. The squid makes a superb visual attractor and also helps a soft worm stay on the hook during casting.*

• *Some anglers stuff the body of squid with enticing titbits such as pieces of peeler crab or mashed up mackerel. Once the body is filled, you whip it with thread or elastic and hook it in the normal fashion. It's best to make these squid parcels at home and then freeze them.*

• *If you're using frozen squid, make sure you give it time to thaw out naturally. Putting the frozen squid into water simply dissipates the smell and makes them less effective. Any unused, defrosted squid should be thrown away at the end of the trip. It won't refreeze naturally.*

• *Don't be in too much of a hurry to throw away the head of a squid if you're making strips. It can prove a top bait for smaller fish with its smell and succulence; even mullet may be tempted.*

Victoria and Battery piers. Douglas Head is a popular mark for whiting and coleys, especially in the winter. The Loch is popular after heavy winds for dogfish, flatfish and codling. Boat fishing can also be successful. There are some tope, along with good skate and conger.

On the south coast, Port St Mary offers some tremendous and varied sport. For the visitor, you can concentrate on the wrasse from the rocks and the pier. You should also be in luck with flatfish and some mackerel – all accessible from the pier itself. The boat fishing, too, is first rate, with tope, cod, conger and skate. Port St Mary is generally considered the hotspot for sea angling on the island and it fishes well into the winter, with plenty of coalfish down by the front wall. Fish light for the best results.

On the west side of the island, Peel offers another hotspot. It fishes well during the holiday season, from both the beach and the breakwater. Expect mackerel and all manner of flatfish, along with some dogfish. There is rock fishing available and this offers good pollack fishing. In the winter, the breakwater also yields plenty of coalfish and the promenade is good after a spell of north-westerly winds, again for coalfish and a few flounder. These can be of good size.

Situated near the northern tip of the island is the famous Manx match. To find this, take the A10 from Ramsey to Bride and turn right at the roundabout close to the church. Move onto the A16 and head for the Point of Ayr. Look for the landfill tip and you will find a track that leads down to the car-park. This is generally regarded as the best match venue on the Isle of Man, especially in the summer months. It is popular for locals and visitors alike. Dogfish are one of the main target species here. It's rumoured that you're going to have to expect at least five fish an hour to be in with a chance of winning! The best fishing is at low water and this avoids struggling with the strong tides that move round the Point of Ayr itself. During the summer, especially early on, the fisherman can also expect a few bull huss. These are rare, but reach double figures when you find them.

⊨ **ACCOMMODATION** – contact the Isle of Man Tourist Department on 01624 686766 for more details on the wide variety of accommodation.

⟳ **TACKLE SHOPS** – tackle shops will provide bait and information on the best skippers. Contact Hobby Time on 01624 625720, Intersport on 01624 674444 and the Tackle Box on 01624 836343 at Foxdale. Phone the Ramsey Warehouse on 01624 813092 for information on competitions and up-to-the-minute advice on bait and methods.

SEA-FISHING SITES
IN SCOTLAND

I never realised before moving up here twenty or so years ago how immense the Scottish sea-fishing scene actually is. You've got a huge, heavily indented coastline with a never-ending number of bays, rocky headlands, sea lochs, wrecks, islands, sandy beaches, fertile worm beds – just about everything imaginable. Add to that the warm waters of the Gulf Stream and the very cold depths of the far north and it really does have an almost frightening amount on offer. To my mind, there are all sorts of sea fishing that you can target. First of all, there's all the general sort of angling available – great cod, pollack and haddock. After that you've got the truly magnificent fish – the fish of your dreams perhaps. For example, huge skate from places such as Loch Aline, giant porbeagles off the north coast and there is even a rumour of blue-fin tuna coming back along the shores of the north west. These are big fish that can barely be matched anywhere else in the world.

CHRISTOPHER WEST, EX-FISHERY SCIENTIST, NORTH UIST

I couldn't agree more with Christopher but, in my own experience, there is another aspect of sea fishing round Scotland that he hasn't covered – light-line fishing. You can fish for bass and sea trout in innumerable rocky coves, both on the mainland and out on the islands themselves. You will also find wrasse amongst the kelp and the rocks. There are even large shoals of mullet that patrol many areas throughout the summer. These can be very big fish indeed, even this far north, and, like the bass and the sea trout, demand a specialised, thoughtful approach. So, you can catch mackerel off a summertime pier, stalk bass in crystal-clear sea pools or set out on a serious boat in the depths of winter for a porbeagle shark, weighing anything in excess of 500 pounds. When it comes to sea fishing, Scotland really does have the lot.

BALCARY FLAT ROCK

Let's start with a look at the well-known Balcary Flat Rock, near Auchencairn on the west coast. This is a great area for the visiting angler, and the village of Auchencairn is a timeless little place that is loved by visitors. It's a typical old fishing village that was once a centre for serious smuggling activities. Nowadays the money of the village comes from bed and breakfast rather than imported rum.

To find Balcary Flat Rock, take the Solway coast road (the A711) out of Dalbeattie. In a few miles, you will come to the coastal village of Auchencairn. Turn left at the War Memorial and follow the signs for the Balcary Bay Hotel. Go down a single-track road until you come to the hotel car-park. From here, go right and you will see a signpost for Balcary Point and Rascarrel. It is a fifteen–twenty minute walk from there to the mark, through fields and countryside. You will then see the Flat Rock itself, with its wooden monument. The pathway down to the Rock isn't too difficult and you will find comfortable fishing into deep water and over clear ground. The easiest fishing is at slack water – during the ebb and flow strong currents can prove a problem. Locals fish this area in the winter, often during tough weather, for cod, but, as a visitor, I'd suggest great caution. This is very much a place for the summer angler to enjoy some stunning scenery.

The winter cod can really be something special – double-figure fish are not uncommon – but let's forget these for the moment and bear the visitor in mind. Spring sees some thornback rays but, as the weather warms, anything can take the bait. You can expect flatfish (including flounder, plaice and dab), bull huss and dogfish. There are also some very good conger around. Big bunches of lobworm are an obvious favourite for the winter cod. In the summer, smaller worm baits will pick up the flatfish. Mackerel is a good bait for the conger and the thornback.

The Rock is the prime mark in the area but there are other rocky points about that all demand a bit of investigation.

⊨ ACCOMMODATION – contact the Tourist Information Centre in Dumfries on 01387 253862.

○ TACKLE SHOPS – the local tackle shops are McCowan's in Dalbeattie on 01556 610270 and Mitchell's in Kirkcudbright on 01557 330426. There's also a sea-angling club in Kirkcudbright; contact Stewart Ross on 01557 330845.

OBAN

Let's now look at a real jewel, the Argyllshire town of Oban. This is a fabulous town set amongst stunning scenery. It's a world of glens, forests, lochs and streams, and, of course, amazing sea fishing. Oban buzzes with charter-boat traffic. It's an area of hugely deep water and many, many islands. The Sound of Mull, the Firth of Lorne, Innish, Back Islands – legendary places. The common skate hereabouts grow to 200 pounds or more, making Oban the skate centre of Europe. Mind you, there's an awful lot more on offer – thornback, ling, doggies, spur dog, conger, cod, tope, even a few hake. Get out to the islands and drift close to the rocks and you'll even start picking up some tremendous ballan wrasse. Expect pollack in deeper water and, throughout the high summer months, big runs of mackerel.

But let's have a look at what makes Oban truly great – the skate. Most of the skate fishing takes place over very deep water – expect to be fishing a hundred yards plus. There is water going down to more than double that and that's sometimes where the very biggest fish live. So you'll have a real fight on your hands.

March, April and May seem to be the best months for the really huge fish, which show up on neap tides. But it's all in the lap of the gods. You can charter a boat for a week and get nowhere near fish, especially if you're looking at south-westerly or north-easterly winds.

You'll need a fifty-pound plus rod – some people prefer eighty pounds – and a serious multiplier. Most skippers swear by star drag, as opposed to lever drag, over such deep water. One thing you'll definitely need is a butt pad. A shoulder harness is also advisable. Think in terms of a 250-pound six- or eight-foot mono trace and a 10/0 hook. Two pounds of lead is the norm, but you can double that in a strong tide.

Bait? Some people swear by pollack, but probably all you'll need are a few mackerel. Whole fish are best. Bites are signalled by a prolonged bouncing of the rod tip. Reel in, tighten up and you are about to embark on a gruelling fight. Andy Nicholson has compared it to bringing up a cement mixer! Certainly, it can be heartbreaking to winch a big fish close to the surface, only to have it dive unstoppably back to the depths once again. It's not a task to be undertaken lightly.

Conservation is now a big issue all round Scotland. Photograph your fish certainly, but then make sure it goes back alive. Under no circumstances are these skate to be killed. They might seem thick on the ground, but this is a very specialised and comparatively small environment and the tagging programme seems to suggest that there are not as many fish as one might have originally thought.

ACCOMMODATION – there's a huge amount of accommodation in the Oban area, but two places that are very welcoming to anglers are the Strathnaver Guesthouse on 01631 563305 and the Arbour Bed and Breakfast on 01631 563393. For further information on accommodation, skippers and everything to do with this fabulous area, contact the Tourist Information Board on 01631 563122.

TACKLE SHOPS – try the Anglers' Corner in Oban on 01631 566374.

LOCH ETIVE

Before leaving Oban, let's look at just one more ace up the town's sleeve. The worst wind for the Oban charter boats comes from the north east. This can cause problems as heavy weather begins to hit Loch Linnhe from the direction of Fort William. There is, however, a way round this and local skipper Ronnie Campbell has the answer. He takes his boat up from Oban and heads into the sheltered Loch Etive. This is quite an operation and involves a hair-raising journey over the reef beneath the Connel Bridge. The water can really race out here, so timing is absolutely critical.

Loch Etive is quite a place – a bit of a conundrum for the traditional sea angler. A large part of the loch holds fresh water and, indeed, rainbow trout are actually farmed there. However, as freshwater is less dense, it tends to float on top of the seawater that lies beneath. So, you have a typical Scottish freshwater loch on the surface, but look deeper and you'll find some fantastic sea fishing. Spur dog exist in large numbers, especially in the deeper parts. There are some huge conger, good thornback, cod and pollack. Interestingly, there are hake present as well – not very many, but some very good fish.

Most of those in the know fish quite heavy, generally using braid rather than nylon. This obviously gives greater bite sensitivity and also helps get a fish up from the bottom more quickly. This can be important. The fish population of Loch Etive is a delicately balanced one and Ronnie insists on the vast majority of any catch going back very quickly. The sooner any fish is allowed to return to the depths, the greater its chance of survival.

ACCOMMODATION – see the entry for Oban.

TACKLE SHOPS – contact the Angler's Corner in Oban on 01631 566374.

BOAT HIRE – for charter boats, contact Ronnie Campbell and Donald McClean on 01631 750213 or Adrian Louder on 01631 720262.

GAIRLOCH

Gairloch is a wondrous place, very close to the magical Loch Maree. This is a marvellous area for a family holiday and the fishing, too, is

good. There's plenty of sheltered water close in, offering cod, haddock, mackerel in the summer, pollack and even thornback. There's great fishing to be had further out.

⊢ ACCOMMODATION – the Tourist Information Office on 01445 712130 can advise on accommodation in the area.

○ TACKLE SHOPS – contact West Highland Marine Boats on 01445 712458.

🛥 BOAT HIRE – contact West Highland Marine Boats (see above).

ULLAPOOL

Now we move on up to Ullapool. This, again, is a remote and challenging area, with some extraordinary possibilities. In fact, prominent members of the Angling Writer's Association recently set out from Ullapool on one of the most remarkable of fishing quests. They had information that very big broad bill and great white shark had been seen by commercial net men, some sixty to seventy miles offshore. Great whites are not too concerned about water temperature, as food is the key to their lifestyle. And for food, read seals, especially in the pupping season. The trip, however, was not a success. Any quest like this is heavily dependent on the weather conditions and the winds just blew and blew. Mind you, every great challenge like this takes time and the information they came back with was certainly promising. There is a feeling that white shark are out there to be caught.

For an adventure such as this, you will obviously need the right boat for the job, a skipper with the requisite amount of knowledge and, importantly, the right window in the weather.

⊢ ACCOMMODATION – contact the local Tourist Board on 01854 612135.

○ TACKLE SHOPS – contact Ardmair Point Boat Centre on 01854 612054.

🛥 BOAT HIRE – contact Ardmair Point Boat Centre (see above).

LOCHINVER

Moving up the coast, we come to the busy coastal fishing village of Lochinver. This picturesque little village is perched on the edge of some of the most remarkable scenery of the northern Highlands. The port itself is an absolute hive of activity as boats come and go with their precious cargoes. The fish market really is a sight to behold.

Looking out to sea from Lochinver, you will see Loch Inver in the foreground, which provides a sheltered location for the angler. Lochinver is a spectacular two-hour drive from Inverness.

⊨ ACCOMMODATION – contact the Lochinver Tourist Board on 01571 844330.

○ TACKLE SHOPS – try the Loch Inver Fish Selling Company on 01571 844228

⬅ BOAT HIRE – contact the Loch Inver Fish Selling Company (see above).

THURSO

Let's move now onto the north coast and Thurso. Thurso is situated on the north shore of Pentland Firth, and boasts excellent visitor services for the whole family.

Most boat activity goes out of Scrabster and it was from here that my good friend, Chris Bennett, made history back in the 1990s. Chris is of the old school of sportsmen – a man with huge imagination, colossal dedication and absolutely no fear. Chris talked constantly to the commercial fishermen of the area and began to realise with greater and greater conviction that the Gulf Stream was bringing huge porbeagle along the north coast of Scotland at certain times of the year. His dedication to the job in hand was enormous. Trip after trip was thwarted by appalling weather conditions but Chris persevered, putting up with the six-hour round journey each day back to his home in the great glen.

At last, Chris was successful and after an extraordinary fight of over three hours boated a porbeagle of over 500 pounds. See what I mean about the dramatic side of Scottish sea fishing!

⊨ ACCOMMODATION – contact the Thurso Tourist Board on 01847 892371.

○ TACKLE SHOPS – visit Harper's Tackle Shop in the High Street, on 01847 893179.

⬅ BOAT HIRE – Harper's Tackle Shop (see above) can advise on boat hire.

ORKNEYS, FAROES AND THE WESTERN ISLES

All the islands offer sea fishing of tremendous quality and Orkney, especially, is famous for its huge skate and halibut. And if we want to go even more into the wilds how about the Faroes? These islands were once part of Denmark, but now they are self-governing. They have their own fishery policy and that means a 200-mile limit.

The islands have also got something called the Faroes Bank, one of the most famous cod marks in the entire world. There's no commercial fishing allowed on it, just long-lining and jigging, and even then it gets rested for long intervals. The result – some extraordinary sport with cod of a size unknown in the United Kingdom.

A couple of years ago Bob Brownless mounted his first trip to the Faroes Bank. His team flew from Aberdeen to the islands in the first week of May and then boarded a restored wooden-hold fishing smack, over a

Although other parts of the UK probably enjoy greater numbers of whiting, there are parts of Scotland that see some very good specimens caught – though not often in huge numbers.

• *Possibly the best bait is lugworm, tipped off with squid. Alternatively, try a strip of mackerel doused in pilchard oil.*

• *Whiting and frost are often linked together. This is probably because frost coincides with calm weather – favourite whiting conditions.*

• *Whiting are nocturnal feeders and come close inshore with the onset of darkness.*

• *Whiting are bottom feeders, so make sure that you get your bait down deep. This is very important.*

• *Autumn and early winter often see a major migration of shrimp along the UK shoreline. At this time, shrimp is a great bait for whiting.*

• *Watch the tiny, needle-sharp teeth of the whiting. Use a disgorger or you'll find yourself with many small, painful cuts.*

• *The best period for whiting is probably between October and January – they're certainly at their fittest then.*

• *Whiting don't put up much of a fight on heavy gear simply because of their size. If you can, pursue them with carp gear, or even coarse float-fishing tackle from a boat.*

• *Whiting may appear numerous but we can dent the stocks if we take away unreasonable amounts. Leave the bin liners at home and only take what you can reasonably eat at a sitting.*

• *If there are a lot of whiting around, it often pays to go for a multi-hook one-up-one-down rig. It's not a bad idea to use a strong hook, however, in case you're fortunate enough to hit into a cod.*

• *If you're getting lots of small bites, which are typical of the whiting, leave the rod alone and let the bite develop into a positive pull. If you're using two hooks, you'll often get two fish at a time.*

• *If you're worried about hitting the bites, use lighter tackle. A light bass rod will really show the bites up with startling clarity.*

• *If you catch a two-pound whiting from the shore, you can be a proud angler. A four-pounder from a boat is really something to tell the world about and if you get anything approaching seven pounds, then it's worth checking the record books!*

• *Whiting are very widespread and are caught from Norway as far south as Gibraltar.*

hundred years' old, complete with refitted diesel engine and two masts.

It's about six hours sailing to the Faroes Bank and the lads weren't disappointed. The cod came out in endless numbers and to a really serious size. Many fish of over thirty pounds were taken, although the general feeling was that they had left it just a little bit too late in the year. Probably prime time is February, when the huge females gather on the Faroes Bank to spawn. Bob and his group were predominantly catching males – but of an amazing size. Certainly, in February and March, cod of fifty and even sixty pounds are well on the cards. Fifty-pound outfits are recommended for creatures like this, set up with conventional perch rigs. Big reels are advised – especially over the deeper areas that can go down a hundred yards or more.

There are many other species available on the Faroes Bank – Bob tells me that they landed twenty-three in that one trip alone! Halibut, too, are the thing. Monstrous creatures reaching well over 300 pounds!

The weather, of course, is the key. Bob's initial outing was brought to a swift end by the appearance of a force eleven cyclone! They simply upped and left and spent a very uncomfortable six hours getting back to land. Was it worth it? No-one who has ever been out to the Faroes Bank can ever doubt that, and Bob is more than willing to keep putting groups together to sample what is possibly the best boat fishing anywhere in Europe. I'd give it a go!

But not all the fishing on the islands is done with eighty-pound gear and shoulder harnesses. One of my own favourite destinations is the island of North Uist, easily accessed by car ferry from Oban or Skye or even more quickly by plane from Glasgow.

Uist has a wonderful feel to it – it's like going back to a land forgotten. It's generally low-lying, but there are impressive hills and the inland trout fishing is spectacular.

It is for the bass that you ought to think about Uist. One of the real beauties of the place is that hardly anyone ever fishes for them. One or two locals are in on the secret but, by and large, you'll have this island and its amazing complex of creeks and tidal pools to yourself. Of course, you've got to check out the fishing rights – this is prime sea trout and salmon territory and not all the waters are open. The hotels will be able to advise you.

The bass aren't always large, but they are prolific and they can be taken easily on the fly – very exciting. It's wild, untamed stuff and you really feel like a pioneer. There are also plenty of wrasse found close to the shore in amongst the kelp beds.

ACCOMMODATION – contact the Orkney Tourist Board in Kirkwall on 01856 872856 for further details on accommodation and boat hire in the Northern Isles. In North Uist, try the Loch Maddie Hotel on 01876 500331 or the Langass Lodge Hotel on 01876 580285.

○ TACKLE SHOPS – contact the Orkney Tourist Board (above) or the Western Isles Tourist Centre in North Uist on 01876 500321.

🚤 BOAT HIRE – for trips to the Faroe Islands, contact Bob Brownless at Bobsport on 01313 326607.

ABERDEENSHIRE

Moving south towards Aberdeen you will meet with a stern, unremitting coastline that, in truth, doesn't do a great deal for the visiting summer tourist. This is more a land of strenuous cod fishing during the winter months. The area demands a really positive approach – and that's putting it mildly – especially when north-easterly winds thrash the shoreline.

Stonehaven, which has several boats covering good rough ground, produces cod, plaice, haddock and ling. There are also some wrecks that can produce very good cod fishing.

Further south, one of the best places to look at is Inverbervie, which is one of the really notorious cod marks on the Aberdeenshire coast. It's got a lot going for it. The beach is only about a quarter of a mile long, but it's an end-to-end hotspot, with some good, deep water very close in. Moreover, there are no problems with accessibility. The beach is very close to the main street and you can almost fish from the car itself – something that makes it popular with visitors and locals alike, especially in tough weather, which is frequent. Big gales obviously dislodge a lot of food and attract good cod – often into double figures – in close. However, you've got to be wary of your own safety and look out for heavy swells or dislodged shingle. Really heavy water can cause a problem with uprooted weed as well. Perhaps it is best – for fishing and for safety – to concentrate on the back end of bad weather.

The cod season starts in early November generally and runs through to February, with the mid-period usually considered the best. Of course, it's all weather-dependent and you do need rough weather to get those fish moving and feeding close in. Don't worry too much about night fishing – daytime can also be good, especially on the last three hours of the flood and an hour over the top. Go for big baits and tackle suited for a very tough job indeed.

🛏 ACCOMMODATION – contact Tourist Information in Stonehaven on 01569 762806.

○ TACKLE SHOPS – contact Fraser's Fishing Tackle in Aberdeen on 01224 590211.

🚤 BOAT HIRE – contact A. Troup on 01569 62892, A. Mackenzie on 01569 63511, W. Lawson on 01569 63565 and J. Lobban on 01569 65323.

SEARCHING OUT THE BASS

In Scotland, you may well find yourself on your own when it comes to fishing for bass. All that shoreline, with hardly any anglers, should be a delight – but where on earth do you start?

• Bass feed on prawns, shrimps, sand eels, crabs, worms, small fish and so on, so look for areas where foodstuff is likely to live.

• Favourite areas are big rock outcrops. These give cover and protection for the foodstuffs we're talking about.

• Look also for weed patches on large boulders – very good starting points.

• Big rock pools hold all the foodstuffs we've just mentioned when they are stranded by the falling tide. Bass will look for these areas as the water begins to seep in again.

• Look for seemingly insignificant inlets between steep-sided cliffs. These are important collecting points for food items. The cliffs themselves provide cover for the bass.

• Look for areas of shallow, muddy or sandy water where worms thrive. Bass like warm water and shallows heat up quickly.

• Watch for areas where the tide's current is at the strongest and the waves are more turbulent – this is where bass will find their food.

• You'll need to do most of your searching at low tide. Take a pencil and pad with you so you can make a quick map of all the promising points that you find.

• Always check the tide table before going out to look for new marks. Leave for high ground the very moment the tide starts to come in and make sure that it doesn't cut you off.

• Don't go out if it's wet. Weeds and boulders can turn to glass under moisture. Watch out for dangerous holes and crevices.

• Avoid steep cliffs. Look for a safe way down or forget them altogether.

• Try not to go out alone – it's important to have a friend with you for safety's sake.

• Try to get out on dawn or dusk tides when the weather is calm. You sometimes see bass hunting on the surface.

• Take a pair of binoculars with you at such times so that you can scan large areas of coastline.

• Take as little gear as possible when fishing. That way you are very mobile and can search out as much new territory as possible.

• If you can find local advice, use that as a starting point and add your own experiences to it as you go.

FIFESHIRE

Let's move down the coast now to Fife, an area that offers really good
sea- fishing opportunities, especially to those holidaying in Edinburgh.
The capital, of course, is a stunning city, with plenty of restaurants,
shopping, and places of historical interest.

North of Edinburgh, but well within driving distance, we come to
Dysart Harbour. This is an appealing place and has the advantage of the
piers that surround the harbour, an area that gives good access. For the
visitor, you'll find some quite good mackerel fishing through July and
August. It's not a long season, but the fish can be prolific. There are also
some good flounder available, although the very big fish tend to show up
from September onwards. This, however, is a popular mark for locals in
the winter when the codling fishing can be excellent, along with a better
class of flounder. For the mackerel, try lightish spinning tackle first. You
might need quite a heavy lure to cast a decent distance. The fish often do
hang further out. For flounder in the summer, try to get crabs if you can
– very much a favourite here. You'll find plenty of parking available
around the harbour.

Ravenscraig Castle is also a good centre on the Fife coast and just
south of there you'll find Kirkcaldy. As on much of the Fife coastline,
you'll find a lot of broken ground here, with some rough patches. These
are the marks where the locals target cod throughout the autumn and
winter. You'll run up against some bass and quite a number of flounder
in the summer. So watch out for snags and use a rotten bottom to avoid
constant, complete break-offs.

⊨ ACCOMMODATION – contact the Tourist Information Centre in Kirkcaldy on 01592 267775.

○ TACKLE SHOPS – in Kirkcaldy, try We're Game on 01592 654301 and Spike's Plaice on
01592 597231, and in Buckhaven, try Intersport on 01592 712480.

SEA-FISHING SITES IN NORTH-EAST ENGLAND

EDINBURGH
Dunbar
St Abb's Head
Eyemouth

NORTH
SEA

Berwick-upon-Tweed

Peebles
Galashiels
Coldstream
Holy Island
Budle
Seahouses
Embleton Bay
Craster Skeers

Farn
Deeps

SCOTLAND

A72
A1
A68

Jedburgh
Alnmouth
Coquet Island
Warkworth
Amble
Creswell Creswell Skeers
Lynemouth
Newbiggin-by-the-Sea
Blyth

Foreshore
Sand bank

N

Otterburn
The Border
A697
A1

Morpeth
Cambois

NORTHUMBERLAND
Ponteland
NEWCASTLE UPON TYNE
River Tyne
Black Middens Rocks
South Shields
Whitburn
Washington
Sunderland
Roker Pier (Sunderland)

Durham
Peterlee

DURHAM
Hartlepool
Bishop Auckland
Stockton-on-Tees
Redcar
Redcar Scars
Saltburn-by-the-sea
Skinningrove
Port Mulgrave
Saltwick Bay
Whitby
Robin Hood's Bay

Darlington
Middlesbrough

Scotch
Corner

North York Moors
Hayburn Wyke
Scarborough
Filey
Filey Brigg
Filey Bay
Flamborough Head

Thirsk
A170
Malton

NORTH
YORKSHIRE
Ripon
Bridlington

Skipton
Harrogate

A1
A65
A59

EAST RIDING OF
YORKSHIRE

York
Tadcaster
Market
Weighton
Beverley

BRADFORD
LEEDS
KINGSTON-UPON-HULL

WEST YORKSHIRE
Hessle
Paull
Withernsea
Huddersfield
Barton-upon-Humber
Humber Bridge
Old Hall
Wakefield
Thorne
Immingham
River Humber
Spurn Head
Barnsley
Scunthorpe
Grimsby
Cleethorpes
Doncaster

SHEFFIELD

SOUTH
YORKSHIRE
Louth
Mablethorpe

Lincoln
Horncastle
Ingoldmells
Skegness

LEICESTERSHIRE
Coningsby

‘The future up here is really buoyant for both shore and charter fishing. We're going through a real boom time and seem to be doing a lot better than many, if not most, places. We hardly ever experience total blanks. There are times when we absolutely bag up with codling, along with some coleys and pollack. The winter shore fishing, too, is magnificent. If you get the slightest bit of wind, this coast is second to none. All the beaches fish with a sea on. You can catch off sandy beaches with anything like a wind, otherwise look out for the rock ends amongst the kelp beds. Expect fish between two and eight pounds, with the bigger fish coming off the shore with the sea running. I recently went out with a friend and we caught ten fish of between two and a half and nine pounds, all on cocktails of white worm, lug and crab. I ought to add that the summer fishing is increasingly good. However, this seems to be a sport reserved for the visitors – historically, fishermen up here aren't sport anglers, but simply fish for the pot. I guess they need a bit of education as to what total sea fishing is all about.’

BOB WHITE, AMBLE SKIPPER AND TACKLE SHOP OWNER

The north east has traditionally been a coast for hard men, guys who work long hours and who feel they can justify their sport if they take home some fresh fish for the table. Fine, but history can be re-written and, as Bob says, the summer sport along this coastline is coming along in leaps and bounds. There used to be the odd bass or two, but now there are plenty between two and even five or six pounds. You can get them on float-fished or legered ragworm. A lot come from the beaches on bait intended for flatfish. There are even mullet now as well. In fact, commercial net men say they get as many mullet as salmon and sea trout. So, whether it's winter codling or summer bass and mullet that you want to target, this is a real up-and-coming area.

BERWICK-UPON-TWEED

The area from Berwick-upon-Tweed to St Abbs Head is well known for codling. You'll also pick up great bags of cod, pollack, ling and wrasse off shore. Berwick-upon-Tweed itself is a great town for holidaying, full of romance, history and natural beauty. It sits just south of the Scottish border, proudly and defiantly offering a whole lot to the sea angler.

If you go out of the town towards the north, you will find high cliffs and rugged rocks everywhere. Moving south, you will find some rock and also plenty of sandy beaches. If you're thinking of shore fishing, the rocks offer some very good wrasse and, at times, you will find both bass and mullet.

If you can bring your own boat up, then you'll be in for some great sport offshore. Contact the Harbour Master, Captain Peter Blanche, on 01289 307404 for details of the local slipway, which is on the southern side of the Tweed close to the lifeboat station.

ACCOMMODATION – contact the local Tourist Board in Berwick-upon-Tweed on 01289 330733.

TACKLE SHOPS – contact Gamefare on 01289 305119.

BOAT HIRE – contact David Thompson, skipper of *On A Promise*, on 01289 302749.

NORTH NORTHUMBRIA

The extreme north east, south of Berwick, is fertile ground for cod, flatfish and coleys. Holy Island, Budle and Seahouses all offer some great fishing. Embleton Bay produces cod, flounder and pollack. Try evening tides in particular. Try Warkworth for flatfish on rag, lug and strips of fish. Night fishing on the beach is especially productive for cod and codling.

However, Amble, one of the jewels of the Northumberland coast, is particularly worth a try. Amble has a commercial history and the harbour was built back in early Victorian times to convey coal from the local mines. The port was closed in the 1960s as the coal industry declined, but later years have seen a great deal of development. A marina and an active boatyard all give the impression of a bustling town that is going places.

Amble has a reputation for boat fishing and large catches of cod. One of the great bonuses of the place is that you don't have to steam for hours to find the fishing grounds. The cod come in close, indeed you can find them on the doorstep. Expect big catches of cod at good times of the year, especially if the season is half kind. It's not unusual for a boat to take over a hundred fish.

You'll also be catching coalfish, pouting, wrasse, ling and, possibly, some mackerel. So you can expect a good mixed bag and some good close-in fishing. The best-known local marks are Cresswell Skeers, Craster Skeers, Coquet Island and North and South Bay.

Amble is also a centre for some tremendous bass fishing. North-East England isn't renowned for the species but Amble is a great place to start for this most desirable of fish. You probably won't be getting super-big specimens, but, with a good number of fish between three and four pounds, this is hardly an issue. Look for them north of the town, all the way to Alnmouth. You can fish for them from the shore, and try fishing at low tide with ragworm. You'll also pick up flounder, turbot and dab, which are prolific in the area. The exposed South Pier at Amble also produces smaller fish, especially in rougher weather – if you can take the exposure! Cliff House and the paddling pool promenade behind the pier also give plenty of bass, especially during the summer time. Try crab for the best results.

Amble is also one of the best areas for mackerel fishing along the north east. The South Pier has always been a focus for mackerel, and though results aren't anything like what they used to be in the past, it is still well worth the effort. Look for the flattest possible seas and an early morning or evening high tide. Try using float-fished mackerel strips, feathers or just single spinners. If there are a lot of fish and you don't want to take that many, snip off a couple of the hook points to make return much easier. Be conservation-minded, and make sure that all fish that aren't required for eating or bait are returned at once and as gently as possible. Stocks are on the way back, so let's not deplete them.

Amble is also a major centre for open competitions. The big one, the Amble Open, takes place early in the year and has in the past attracted up to a 1000 competitors. However, there are many club matches fished around Amble during the summer months, which always prove an additional attraction for the visitor.

Perhaps Amble rings a bell with you... Well, it was in the national news back in the late 1990s with Freddie the dolphin – an enchanting creature that made its way to the area, liked what it saw and decided to stay for a while. He soon became something of a local celebrity and the local boatmen, always with an eye to a profit, began taking tourists out for a viewing. I suppose the fact that Freddie stuck around speaks volumes about the amount of fish available in the area.

Moving south, Druridge Bay fishes well for flatfish, codling and the odd bass. Cresswell, Lynemouth, Newbiggin and Cambois are all worth visits. Expect several species, notably the occasional big cod.

⊨ ACCOMMODATION – there's a wide variety in the area – phone the Tourist Information Centre in Amble on 01665 712313.

○ TACKLE SHOPS – Amble Angling Centre, 4 Newburgh Street, Amble on 01665 711200 is a mine of information, with excellent tackle and bait available. Boat trips can also be arranged from the shop.

◞ BOAT HIRE – try Bob White on 01665 711200, Micky Potts on 01665 575731, Jim Kelly on 01665 711008, Dave Builth on 01665 712561 or Andy Toward on 0191 2863848. If you're in the area on holiday, it might be worth contacting David Grey on 01665 712313 – he takes trips to the Cockett Island Bird Reserve every day. The island is famous for its puffins, eider duck and flocks of terns.

BLYTH

Blyth is our next port of call – a once thriving port and still a major centre for sea fishing. The Blyth estuary and river are both very heavily fished throughout the summer and winter alike – a good area for experienced anglers and beginners. The port itself is protected from the north-east side by the Cambois Pier, now out of bounds for anglers but still offering protection from severe north-easterlies. The South Pier, however, is open to anglers and is a good fishing area, both in daylight and darkness. It has wooden piles and you can catch by either dropping down or distance casting. You get to the pier through the south harbour – just a five-minute walk. Expect cod and coalfish in the winter, with some good plaice during May and June. You will find it very busy in July and August when the schools break up and the mackerel arrive in even greater numbers than the children! You'll pick mackerel up between one and two pounds, on either light spinning tackle or float fishing with a smidgen of fish strip for bait. Expect good sport at high water, dawn and dusk.

Peeping Tom's Rocks, just inside the mouth of the Blyth estuary, is a favourite area. It is only accessible two and a half hours either side of low water by means of the small beach. Make sure you get your timings right. When you're casting from the rocks, the bait will go straight into the river's main channel. The fish feed well when the water is on the move, especially from dusk into darkness. Expect large shoals of coalfish through the autumn and winter, with a few codling.

The Blyth Quayside is located very near the centre of Blyth itself and you can actually drive to the area, making it popular with the casual fisherman and just about everyone else when the river is foul.

Bate's Jetty, actually composed of a series of wooden jetties, is also a favourite area and makes casting into the main channel easy. You will find the area down a small dirt track behind the Golden Fleece pub. You've only got to cast fifteen yards or so and you'll be in the main channel, once again amongst big numbers of codling and coalfish.

It's also worth looking at the area between the marina up to Black Bridge. This constitutes the upper reaches of the Blyth, which, at low water, is a network of mudflats and channels. It's best fished in the summer for flounder and eels. High water is the best time. The fish that live in the inaccessible channels now fan out over the mudflats feeding hard. Fish light with worm or peeler crab to get the best of the sport.

⊨ ACCOMMODATION – contact the Tourist Information Office in Newcastle on 0191 2610610.
⊙ TACKLE SHOPS – contact Sport and Leisure in Blyth on 01670 365980.

THE RIVER TYNE

On our southward journey, we inevitably come to Newcastle and the River Tyne. Newcastle is a hotbed of enthusiasm – for culture, music, soccer and sea fishing. The town is centre to a major sea-fishing brotherhood and local competitions are phenomenally well attended. The Tyne offers a huge amount of fishing possibilities. The shore fishing at the mouth of the river is made extra special by the two piers that jut out, giving shelter to the inner harbour.

The pier at South Shields is a real favourite, open all year round, apart from during severe weather conditions. It fishes particularly well during the winter, with terrific catches of cod and coalfish. In fact, it's probably the hottest mark in the north east. In summer, the pier is equally popular with youngsters and visitors who catch good numbers of mackerel and launce sand eels. Depending on the weather, these flock the river from July through to the middle of August. Access to the North Pier is much more restricted and is generally only allowed to local clubs for pre-arranged matches. But, if you can get there, expect some very good cod, coalfish and flatfish.

Sticking with the shore fishing, see if you can get to Black Middens Rocks. These constitute a notorious shipping hazard, but at low water they are massively productive for the fisherman. Expect good bags of cod and coalfish, along with some really top quality flounder. For bait, try peeler crab or lugworm.

The lower estuary absolutely bristles with jetties and fishing possibilities. However, as Newcastle's prosperity expands and development marches forwards, the number of jetties open to the angler is necessarily declining. This is, obviously, a great shame, but it does mean that pressure on stocks is more limited. On the north bank of the estuary, the prime area for anglers is the open Fish Quay between the Fish Market and the Ice Store. Look next at the old Smith Docks or the Bergen Quay. You'll pick up the usual bags of cod, coalfish and flounder, along with eels at certain times of the year. This is good fishing, but long casting out into the main channel generally gives the best results. On the south side of the lower estuary, try the Groyne, Mill Dam and the Velva Liquids Jetty.

Don't ignore the upper estuary either. This is particularly productive during the summer for flounder and eels. Newcastle Quayside has been renovated with anglers in mind and there is a mass of fishing opportunities. The Walker Riverside Park is also a hot area – watch out for abandoned shopping trolleys, however!

For those wishing to go afloat, Newcastle-upon-Tyne is a real haven. The port is home to any number of experienced charter skippers who have been working the inshore waters and the offshore wrecks for their entire lives. You'll generally be offered an inshore trip, going some twelve miles out. Alternatively, you may like to try a trip to the Graveyard, which is three times the distance. The skippers know which is best at any one particular time, so be guided by them. There's a proliferation of wrecks out there. Be warned though – they're all home to monster fish.

Moving further south, Whitburn is a delightful small village situated between Newcastle and Sunderland, but still maintaining a pleasant, rural feel to it. The fishing can also be good, especially for codling and the odd bigger cod.

⊨ ACCOMMODATION – accommodation is widespread, as you'd expect in such a large area. The nearest Tourist Information Office can be contacted on 0191 2610610.

○ TACKLE SHOPS – try Billy's on 0191 2596262, ID Fishing on 0191 2763041, John's Fishing Tackle on 0191 2343412, Reelsports on 0191 4300247, Steve's Tackle on 0191 2579999, Walker Tackle Shop on 0191 2764774, Two Jacks Fishing Tackle on 0191 2345640 and the Country House on 0191 2616669. Apart from selling bait, tackle, clothing and all the necessities, these shops will also advise on local charter skippers.

⮑ BOAT HIRE – for direct contacts, try Jim Rutherford on 0191 4832745, George Skinner on 0191 2657288 and Alan Skinner on 0191 2764863.

THE RIVER WEAR

Inevitably, we now come to Sunderland and the River Wear. There are plenty of piers in the area – four alone around the mouth of the River Wear – and they all offer distinct possibilities. Of them all, perhaps Roker Pier, the most northerly one, is the favourite simply because it offers tremendous sport summer and winter alike. It's a popular venue throughout the season, but is especially patronised during the autumn and winter codding. But, for the summer tourist, there's plenty of activity with dab, plaice and flounder, especially when you cast into

England international Jim Whippy holds up a superb bass. These buccaneering fish visit our waters from spring right through to winter, often coming close inshore.

Many species will take a plug, spinner or plastic lure, but few as ferociously as the bass. A diving plug like this works well in clear water close to the shore or among rocks.

The rolling Atlantic surf off the west coast of Ireland is bound to have all bass anglers drooling. For years, beaches like this have received avid pilgrims from all over Europe.

A glorious view as the sun begins to sink. The rugged north-west coast of Scotland offers unparalleled fishing opportunities, largely because of the lack of angling pressure.

Jim Pressley, renowned world boat-fishing champion, holds a couple of superb rays. Generally caught offshore, they can sometimes be taken in close, especially at night.

the harbour side of the breakwater. Summer also sees mackerel shoals coming in – great fun on light spinners or feathers. If you really enjoy mackerel fishing – and who doesn't – try float fishing for them on coarse gear with perhaps just a sliver of fish as bait. Use four-pound line or so and you will certainly have a fight to remember.

In the winter, lugworm is the top bait for the cod, but peeler crab works well throughout the year – if you can get it that is! Another local tip is to fish for the prolific whiting with lugworm that has been tipped with a trace of squid or mackerel.

Just a word of caution: towards the end of the pier you will come across quite a few snags so it's wise to fish with a rotten bottom so you can pull easily for a break. There's also a difficult area halfway along called the Barrier. However, this area of rock and weed produces some of the best fish! Isn't that always the case?

The pier offers free fishing but it is closed during severe weather conditions, generally in winter. You will find a free car-park close by, along with a pub and café serving refreshments.

◖ ACCOMMODATION – accommodation isn't quite as prolific as you'll find further up on the Tyne, but there's still a good spread. Phone the Sunderland Tourist Information Office on 0191 5532000/1.

○ TACKLE SHOPS – the local tackle shop is Rutherford's and they keep a good supply of fresh bait. Contact them on 0191 5654183.

HARTLEPOOL TO SALTBURN-BY-THE-SEA

Moving south again, Hartlepool is another favourite area, especially for codling. Redcar Scaurs is always worth a try for codling, particularly when the weather is rough. Saltburn-by-the-Sea is one of the major centres of this particular area. This is a serene and small seaside town that really comes to the fore during the winter. It's a major area for both winter cod and, especially, whiting, which come in huge numbers during the autumn. The best spot, by far, is the end of the town's pier. It's not unusual to see catches exceed twenty fish, with some of them being in the two-pound bracket. You'll also pick up the odd flatfish and bass, with mackerel shoaling during the summer.

About a quarter of a mile to the right of the pier, just by the cliffs, you'll come across a patch of rough ground and a deep gully called Penny Hole. This is another top winter mark renowned for holding large cod – some into double figures. Night fishing, as so often, pays dividends, especially at low water when you can get a bait right into the Hole. It's

ROCK FISHING

Although the north east is not quite as blessed with rocks as say Devon and Cornwall, there are still good rocky areas, notably Filey Brigg. Rock fishing, however, is a skill all of its own.

• Safety must always govern your choice of venue. Pay particular attention to weather conditions and the state of the tide. If you are a stranger to the area, ALWAYS check with the locals on matters of safety. At best, you might have to sit marooned on a rock for a few hours while the tide recedes. The worst doesn't bear thinking about.

• It's always good to wear flotation aids. In winter, these can help retain body warmth, as well as perhaps saving your life if you should slip.

• Conger eels inhabit rocky areas and you can often catch them close in, especially when the water is coloured after a blow. If your fishing is restricted to daylight hours, go for cloudy days when there's a good wind.

• Calm settled weather is good for wrasse.

• Wrasse are a great rock species – full of fight and startling to look at. You can fish for them with any tough coarse-fishing gear, but a good bass rod often provides extra length and power. Even a three-pound fish takes some subduing. Don't tackle them with less than a twelve-pound line.

• If you're fishing in the rocks for big fish species, don't consider going light. A big multiplier such as the Abu 9000, with two-speed gearing and a tough drag, is the sort of reel you're looking at; thirty-pound line is an absolute minimum. Rods must match – go for powerful tournament casters, not beach rods as these won't give you that added spine.

• Back to safety: make sure that your fishing platform is way above the range of any rogue swell that could come along. Make sure that you can land a fish easily and without danger. Always check that your emergency exit is easily found and accessible – especially in the dark.

• Wherever possible, study your rocks carefully, especially at low water, which gives you a better idea of the ground you're fishing over.

• For the holidaying angler, daylight fishing is the most likely option. This is where wrasse come into their own. Try float fishing for them as this drifts the bait in and out of crevices that legering can't reach. If you're going to fish a static bait on the lead, try touch legering. Bites are generally very bold.

• Wrasse are also very obliging for the holiday angler – they start appearing around most of our shoreline in the late spring and are present throughout the summer. For bait, try either crab or lugworm.

good to watch where the locals are going at this particular time because it's not always easy to locate the gully. Also, ask advice about the tides as it's easy to get cut off. Close to Penny Hole is the Ship pub – an excellent area for bass in the two- to four-pound mark.

To the left of the pier, you will find shallow, sandy flats, which look absolutely featureless but, surprisingly, can pay dividends through the winter. The secret is the sandbank that is located about a hundred yards out, running parallel to the beach. If you can get a bait the other side of this feature you'll hit straight into codling. Expect also some bass – schoolies primarily during the summer, but some big fish through the winter and into early spring. Ten-pounders are not that uncommon.

⊨ **ACCOMMODATION** – contact the Hartlepool Tourist Information Centre on 01429 869706.

○ **TACKLE SHOPS** – contact Cairns Angling in Hartlepool on 01429 272581.

SKINNINGROVE

Moving into North Yorkshire, we come to the old industrial town of Skinningrove. This town has a pier built about a hundred years ago at the behest of the local iron and steel industry. Over the years, heavy seas and neglect have destroyed a good part of the pier, and walkers and fishermen can no longer use its entire length. There is still, however, a good amount remaining, and the area around the Gate – the cut-off point – is renowned for flounder, whiting and some big cod. There is year-round sport of the highest quality.

The beach at Skinningrove is also top quality. Flounder and whiting are caught year round on light tackle. Long casting isn't necessary and you'll pick up codling in the late winter and early spring. Lugworm is the killing bait, especially tipped with mussel, squid or mackerel.

Moving further along, you'll come to an area of rocky coastline and the first important mark, Hummersea Steps. This is a well-known area for cod, with some big fish, along with pouting and plenty of rockling.

As a general rule, try to fish the pier in darkness. A spring tide is particularly productive. A north-east or north-west swell also helps matters. Hummersea Steps is a high-water venue, especially in rough conditions when there's a north-westerly blowing.

⊨ **ACCOMMODATION** – contact the Hartlepool Tourist Information Centre on 01429 869706.

○ **TACKLE SHOPS** – the local tackle shop, Keith's Sports on 01287 624296, will provide all the information that you're likely to need. It's also worth contacting the Skinningrove Angling Club on 01287 639572 for further information and possible membership

PORT MULGRAVE

Just a little way down the coast from Skinningrove, we come to Port Mulgrave, another really fabulous mark. An old and now disused stone jetty is central to the fishing at Port Mulgrave. The jetty is surrounded by rocky outcrops and slate ledges. The whole area is a mass of gullies and heavy weed growth – ideal shelter for fish, crab and all the foodstuffs that make up the diet of cod.

Port Mulgrave fishes best at high water from the jetty or low water from the outcrops themselves. Both attacks are successful. You're not going to find a great depth of water around here, and this is one of the reasons most of the locals try to get there by night.

To get down to the sea, you need to go along a winding path that descends the cliff face. It's quite a walk on the way back up, so try to travel as light as you can. Although this is rocky ground, you won't lose too much gear, so don't over-burden yourself.

I've mentioned cod here but you're also likely to pick up eels and coalfish. Peeler crab, mussel and worm are all top baits.

This is a romantic, remote sort of place to fish and it's a good place to get away from the hurly-burly of the bigger cities. And you're in with a chance of catching a double-figure cod to boot.

ACCOMMODATION – details of accommodation available in the area can be obtained from the Tourist Information Centre in Whitby on 01947 602674.

○ TACKLE SHOPS – for more information on the fishing in this area, contact Keith's Sports on 01287 624296 and Whitby Angling Supplies on 01947 603855. The Whitby Angling Club also organises matches here during the winter, mostly in the evenings. They can be contacted on 01947 895429.

WHITBY

Whitby is the next major mark as we proceed south. For many years now, Whitby has been a popular wrecking centre, with charter boats travelling upwards of thirty miles out into the North Sea. There have been some huge catches here – including cod to over fifty pounds, along with haddock, whiting, flatfish, ling and mackerel.

The West Pier is a favourite for locals in the winter and holidaymakers in the summer. There are plenty of flatfish and mackerel for the holiday angler, but you'll find a greater number of codling off the East Pier frequenting the rocky bottom.

Saltwick Bay is another cracking area, found just south of Whitby itself. It fishes particularly well in the winter and has easy access, especially after nightfall when the fishing really picks up. The area generally fishes best when a good sea is running. Apart from cod you'll also pick up flounder and the occasional coalfish.

⊨ ACCOMMODATION – contact the Tourist Information Centre in Whitby on 01947 602674.
○ TACKLE SHOPS – Whitby Angling Supplies on 01947 603855 will provide a host of information on this very popular venue.
⊨ BOAT HIRE – contact John Brennan on 01947 820320. Whitby Charter Skippers Association is also worth contacting for further information. The telephone number is 01609 780412.

HAYBURN WYKE

The next port of call is Hayburn Wyke. This really is a jewel of a place, remote and largely unfished, except by locals. No wonder it was once notorious as a smugglers' cove. It's in the North York Moors National Park and this makes it a particularly serene area. Hayburn Wyke fishes well throughout the year, but, like so many of these coastal venues, it really comes alive in the winter.

The fishing peaks between December and February, as the truly large cod begin to move in. Real monsters – fish of over twenty pounds – have been taken in the past, but the general run is of plentiful smaller fish of four to six pounds.

Locals use cocktails – any combination of worms, crabs or mussels. A long rock rod, a 7000-sized reel and thirty- to forty-pound line will suffice. Don't worry too much about long casting unless the sea is heavy and you've got to get beyond the surf.

Locals swear by a strong south-easterly, and high water is generally considered the top period. However, the covered conditions mean that you can catch fish either day or night. In fact, make sure that you fish the venue during the hours of light at least for your first two or three visits, so that you can familiarise yourself with the surroundings. Never go to a new area for the first time in the darkness.

Hayburn, which is five miles north of Scarborough, takes just a little bit of finding. Find your way to the Hayburn Wyke Hotel and then look for the pathway to the left. This will takes you through the woods and down to the shoreline.

⊨ ACCOMMODATION – contact the Tourist Information Centre in Scarborough on 01723 373333.
○ TACKLE SHOPS – try Buckley's Angling Supplies in Scarborough on 01723 363202.

SCARBOROUGH

Scarborough is another one of the jewels of the Yorkshire coastline, long famous as a major holiday resort, but also offering intriguing possibilities to the sea angler. Most of the year round, the sea fishing is good and can be undertaken from either a charter boat or from the harbour piers.

The West Pier stands on sandy ground, whereas the East Pier, over rock, generally offers the chance of bigger fish, especially cod and codling. The codling usually come in from August onwards – look for numbers of these on the marks north of the town, especially Robin Hood's Bay. The charter boats hereabouts specialise in great catches of cod, especially as the colder months draw on. There are some big fish around.

ACCOMMODATION – as Scarborough is such an important tourist town, there's a great deal of accommodation available. Contact the Tourist Information Centre on 01723 373333.

TACKLE SHOPS – for further information, contact Buckley's Angling Supplies on 01723 363202.

BOAT HIRE – charter boats on offer include the *Valhalla* on 01723 632083, the *Wandering Star* on 01723 374885 and the *Sea Fisher* on 01723 364640.

FILEY AND BRIDLINGTON

Filey has long been a Mecca for sea anglers, especially the famous Filey Brigg, a ridge of rocks running out into deep water and fishable during most tide and weather conditions. This rocky headland offers natural protection to Filey Bay on the south side of the point. Fish the area at night, especially when there's a good northern wind – you'll find that fish are moving onto the worm bed. Flounders are particularly prevalent.

There's a whole host of marks along Filey Brigg – Ben Storeys, Black Hole Corner, High Nab, Green Rock and so on. Ask the locals for advice. Crab is the top summer bait and cocktails take over in the winter. Codling go very well on ragworm and mussel, especially around Christmas time. Make no mistake, Filey really is a prize on this stretch of coastline.

Just south of Filey, you will find Bridlington. The South Pier is a real favourite with holiday anglers. It is free and offers all the usual summer species to keep the irregular sea angler totally involved. The North Pier is only open in the winter when you'll pick up good codling.

Just a word before we leave this very productive area of the Yorkshire coastline. It does produce some tremendous cod fishing throughout the winter months but there is, as ever, a right and a wrong way to go about approaching it. Talk to the locals. Look at their rigs if you can and see what bait they are using. And keep on the move. If you're not getting fish,

RAGWORM

The king ragworm is the most commonly used type of rag in the United Kingdom and attracts just about every fish species that swims. Keeping your rag in perfect condition is quite straightforward. You will usually buy them either in peat or in fine sand. Keep them just slightly damp – a spray bottle filled with seawater is ideal. Wrap them lightly in newspaper and keep them cool – not cold – in the fridge. If that's not possible, then a cold stone floor such as in a garage will serve the same purpose.

• Most rags sold to the angler are between six and eight inches in length – the ideal length.

• Smaller worms will work perfectly in cocktails with crab, shellfish and squid strips.

• Really big worms can be cut into sections.

• If you've got a really big worm, it is best to hook it in the head and fish it on the drift for bass.

• Beads and spoons on the snood above rag help attract flatfish.

• Ragworm are much tougher than lug, and generally prove quite resistant to crabs. However, if you do have any problems, put a few turns of fine elastic thread up and down your baited worm. This will give it extra strength.

• The best hooks are long shank fine or medium wire patterns.

• If you use ragworms extensively, you will find the acidic juices from their bodies will begin to make the flesh on your fingertips sore. To help with any soreness, soak your hands in a bowl of hot water into which you've dissolved half a cupful of salt.

• Harbour ragworm – often called muddies – are a smaller member of the family. They are very good for flounder and mullet. They are also perfect for cocktails with most baits.

• White ragworms are a vital part of the match-fishing scene, as they seem to catch fish under the most impossible of circumstances. These valuable worms are best stored in clean sea-water in a fridge.

• Small whites are best fished in a bunch – perfect for bass and flounder.

• Big whites – snake whites – are the ideal bait for codling after the Christmas period. Don't go without them!

• Always remember that ragworm have a nasty pair of pincers and can give you a good old nip. Beware!

have another battle plan in mind. This means travelling light – a rucksack and perhaps just one rod, a bait bucket and, if you must, a rod rest. During daylight, visit all the areas you might fancy fishing , especially at low water, and look for fish-holding features. The best sea anglers will always have a really good grasp of where they're fishing and what they're doing. Okay, flukes do happen, but for sustained success it's essential to put the time and effort in.

▭ **ACCOMMODATION** – contact the Tourist Information Centre in Filey on 01723 518000.

○ **TACKLE SHOPS** – if you're planning a visit, it makes sense to pick up top quality information from either Filey Fishing Tackle on 01723 513732 or GB Angling in Scarborough on 01723 374017. Filey Brigg Angling Club also is helpful with advice – contact them on 01723 515981.

⬳ **BOAT HIRE** – from Bridlington, many of the boats go out to Flamborough Head or to the wrecks offshore. Contact I. Taylor on 01262 679434 or J. Jarvis on 01262 604750.

SPURN HEAD AND THE HUMBER ESTUARY

Spurn Head is a four-mile spit of land that has been created over the years by coastal erosion. It is the last outpost of Yorkshire, curving into the Humber estuary across the water from Cleethorpes. Spurn Head is a major nature reserve and you'll find a great number of birdwatchers in the area, but there's also some brilliant sea fishing.

It can be fished in most conditions for cod, bass, flounder, along with the odd ray and plaice. There is a toll to get onto Spurn, so take change with you. Also, as the area is heavily frequented by tourists, walkers and birdwatchers, especially on summer weekends, do remember to portray our noble sport to the best of your ability.

It's also worth looking further up the estuary from Spurn Head towards Kingston-upon-Hull itself. The area just downstream of the Humber Bridge isn't the prettiest in the world, and the water itself is all stirred up by passing boat traffic and the influx of major rivers, the Trent especially. The fact the water here never runs clear does at least mean the fish feed well both day and night. Concentrate on the Hessle area – almost in the shadow of the bridge itself. Light gear for flounder and eels is a winner, especially during the summer.

Follow the Clive Sullivan Way eastwards and come off where you see a large Cash and Carry – the Makro mark. This is a favourite area for cod, even though it is snaggy and there's a big drop down to the water.

Moving on down the estuary, Bellway Homes, Paull and Old Hall all have their devotees. All produce good fish, winter and summer alike, though the

HOOK CHOICE

A lot of attention is paid to rods, reels, lines and so on, but it's the hook that makes the first contact with the fish and is probably the item of tackle most likely to let you down. Don't be afraid to ask an experienced skipper for advice. He will welcome that much more than lost fish.
• Sharp, fine wire hooks will penetrate more easily than thick wired hooks. However, fine wire hooks bend under pressure, so you need to think about your target species and your bait. Match anglers are more likely to go for fine wire hooks. Most boat anglers use either medium wire or, occasionally, extra strong, heavy wire hooks. A lot depends on conditions and location.
• You can target a big fish in reasonably shallow, snag-free, calm water on a medium wire hook. Hook that same fish over snags or in deep, turbulent water and you'll have to go for heavy wire.
• Balance the hook to the bait. You need a hook big enough to hold the bait comfortably, but you don't want the hook hidden up by the bait so that it can't penetrate.
• When using large baits, it's a good idea to use bait elastic to tie them to the shank and eye of the hook. This will hold the bait in the position you want it and stop it sliding down towards the point and masking a strike.
• A lugworm on a size 4/0 hook is about right. You could thread four or five lugworms, however, on a 4/0 or 5/0.
• Always keep your hooks dry and corrosion-free.

latter two in particular can take a bit of finding. For Paull, take the signs for Withernsea, look for the signpost, turn right and take the small road until you reach the lighthouse. Note that if you're fishing Old Hall, it's quite a walk. You can't drive down the farmer's tracks to the water, so travel light.

Grimsby has long been a commercial fishing centre, but it also offers excellent possibilities along both the Humber and the foreshore. All the usual species are available, with some good codling, especially in the colder months.

ACCOMMODATION – contact the Tourist Information Centre in Cleethorpes on 01472 323222.

TACKLE SHOPS – for further information, call East Coast Tackle on 01964 535064, Top Sport Angling on 01964 612340, Fred's Fishing Tackle on 01472 352922 or Tight Lines in Cleethorpes on 01472 200400.

SEA-FISHING SITES
IN IRELAND

NORTHERN IRELAND

Inishtrahull

Tory Island

Church Bay · Rathin Island

Portrush

Portstewart · Coleraine

Lough Foyle

Ballycastle

Aran Island

Letterkenny

ANTRIM

Larne

Island Magee

DONEGAL

Ballybofey

Ballymena

Belfast Lough

Donegal

TYRONE

Omagh

Newtownabbey

Bangor

Donaghadee

Cookstown

BELFAST

Newtownards

Donegal Bay

Bundoran

Enniskillen

Portadown

DOWN

Inishmurray

Monaghan

Armagh

Strangford Lough

Portaferry

Inishkea North

Ballina

SLIGO

Sligo

MONAGHAN

Keady

Castlewellan

Inishkea South

Duvillaun More

LEITRIM

Cavan

Newry

Rostrevor

Achill Island

Swinford · Knock Airport

Boyle

Dundalk

Clare Island

Clew Bay

MAYO

Ardee

LOUTH

Clogher Head

Westport

ROSCOMMON

Castlerea

Longford

Drogheda

IRISH SEA

Inishturk

Caher Island

Ballinrobe

Roscommon

WESTMEATH

Navan

Cliden

Tuam

Mullingar

MEATH

Lambay Island

GALWAY

Ballinasloe

Athlone

OFFALY

Edenderry

DUBLIN

Gorumna Island

Galway

Loughrea

Dun Laoghaire

Inishmore

Galway Bay

Naas

Bray

Greystones

Aran Islands

CLARE

REPUBLIC

Ennis

WICKLOW

Wicklow

OF IRELAND

Carrigaholt Bay

Portlaoise

Kilrush

River Shannon

Carlow

Scattery Island

LIMERICK

CARLOW

Smerwick Harbour

Tralee Bay

Fenit

LIMERICK

TIPPERARY

Kilkenny

Ballyferriter

Tralee

WEXFORD

Gt. Blasket Island

Dingle

Castleisland

Tipperary

KILKENNY

Dingle Bay

Mallow

Clonmel

Cahersiveen

Fermoy

Wexford

Valentia Island

KERRY

WATERFORD

Waterford

Waterville

Kenmare

CORK

Scariff

Youghal

Tramore bay

Dursey Island

Bantry

CORK

Kinsale

Bear Island

Courtmacsherry

Clear Island

Nymphe Bank

N

100m 200m 50m 30m

'*As you know, John, I'm primarily a freshwater fisherman for anything that swims over here in Ireland – pike, trout, rudd, even bream and tench, and you'll find me there. But, like many Irishmen, I can't just ignore the quality of the sea fishing that's on offer. It's simply mind-blowing. What's more, you can enjoy a great deal of it using your normal freshwater gear, so you don't have to be involved in a vast amount of expense if you don't want to specialise too much. Mind you, if it's blue-fin tuna that you're thinking of pursuing, that's a different matter altogether! You're not going to land a creature of a 1,000 pounds – and they do grow that big – with freshwater gear are you? And another thing – the coasts of Ireland are simply stunning. You won't see more glorious scenery anywhere in Europe, or the world come to that. See you there!*'

RICHIE JOHNSTON, IRISH ANGLER AND AUTHOR

Richie has been very much my guide when it comes to Irish sea fishing and, like all the Irish, he and his friends have proved an absolute fund of detailed knowledge. But that's what you find wherever you travel in Ireland – hosts of the most genuine hospitality and courteousness. I've been travelling to Ireland since the1960s and, believe me, I've never experienced anything but warmth and welcome. Ireland is the perfect destination for any family looking for unspoilt countryside, peace and relaxation away from the stress of modern rat-race life. For the sea angler, the coastline is awesome. It boasts endless variety and limitless potential. You'll find quaint little villages with welcoming olde-worlde pubs and guesthouses. Just a word about transport. Once, getting to Ireland was something of a haul. Now, numerous low-cost flights and relatively inexpensive car hire make journeys easy and cheap. If you wish to take your own car, the high-speed ferries are highly recommended, especially if you're taking children.

IRELAND

DUBLIN

There are many possibilities around Dublin itself, especially with pollack and wrasse. You can try Dalke Island, which is only fifteen minutes by train from the centre of Dublin. Another possibility is the port of Dun Laoghaire, which offers good pollack and bass opportunities. It also provides pier fishing, with dabs and conger in the summer months. You'll find whiting, codling and coalfish coming in during the winter.

Moving a little way down the coast, you come to Greystones in County Wicklow. To get there, just take the N11 south out of Dublin. There's a little harbour in the village, but if you turn right you'll come to the beach. This used to be one of the centres of Irish cod fishing, but catches have faltered in recent years. The great thing about Greystones – and the reason why it is such a centre for competitions – is the huge amount and variety of fish in the area. You can fish it almost year round, with just a quiet period at the end of the winter. In the summer, codling, bass, coleys, pollack and sea trout all show well. Coleys and codling feature from autumn throughout the winter. All the usual baits succeed – peeler crab, lug, rag, mussels and sand eels. However, don't neglect spinning, especially when the sea is relatively clear. It's a cracking method for sea trout and bass, especially.

Sea trout can be fished all along the south coast, as well as huge shoals of mullet. These seek out any estuary or trickle of fresh water and sometimes you'll find vast shoals, but, as ever, they can be difficult to tempt.

ACCOMMODATION – phone the Tourist Board in Dublin on 00 353 (0)1 6057700.

TACKLE SHOPS – contact Patrick Cleere in Dublin on 00 353 (0)1 6772351.

BOAT HIRE – there are plenty of charter boats available in the area; for details, phone 00 353 (0)404 68751.

CORK AND KINSALE

Cork City itself offers some great sport, both inside and outside the harbour. Kinsale, a little to the west, boasts a fine natural harbour and has been a famous Irish angling centre for many decades. Kinsale is a lovely town with a long-standing fishing history, offering five hotels, at least thirty guest houses and, apparently, over forty pubs and restaurants! So, although the town is small, it has a friendly atmosphere and there's a great deal for everyone to do. The Castle Park Marina fleet is extremely modern. High-speed boats (with a forty-mile offshore licence) mean that anglers can try out several different hot marks in a single day. There's deep water close into the town – twenty minutes or so – so huge amounts of time are not lost in travelling. There are big reefs and plenty of wrecks,

FISHING FOR BALLAN WRASSE

There are several forms of wrasse around the shores of the United Kingdom and Eire. Here, however, I'm going to concentrate on ballan wrasse. They are perfect for the shore angler, especially in areas such as Ireland where there are huge expanses of rocky headland.

• *Ballan wrasse prefer quite shallow water – generally not deeper than forty feet. This means that they will come close inshore.*

• *They like plenty of rocks, boulders and weed. You'll find them in exposed areas – often where you would think they'd get a battering from the wind and swell.*

• *Look for them in the tightest, rockiest, snaggiest, least accessible places! But don't put yourself in any kind of danger.*

• *If you have access to a dinghy, you can often get a boat close inshore under steep rock overhangs where it would be otherwise impossible to fish. The dinghy angler will get the very best out of most rocky headlands.*

• *You can leger for wrasse, but the problem is that the bait will frequently roll into chasms between the rocks. This sometimes means that it is hidden and tackle losses can be very high.*

• *Fishing with a sliding float is a much better idea. Try using a big freshwater float, such as a large Avon or even a small pike float – this slides perfectly up and down the line. A drilled bullet will make it cock and take the bait down.*

• *It's generally unwise to use mainlines of much less than twelve- or fifteen-pound breaking strain. Ballans can grow to nearly ten pounds and they always live in rocky terrain. It's important, therefore, to hit them and hold them from potentially tackle-busting snags. You'll also need a rod that has plenty of backbone to exert the necessary power.*

• *Peeler crab is traditionally one of the great wrasse baits. Wrasse have sharp teeth in their mouth and even stronger teeth in their throat so that they can cope adequately with the toughest of foodstuffs.*

• *If you are using worm – and king rag are very good – try to thread as much of the worm as possible onto the hook bend and shank, leaving very little loose worm hanging off. This helps stop small wrasse shredding the bait completely.*

• *Always be aware of the safety angle. Make sure you know when the tide is going to be in and that you're not going to be marooned. Always look out for a good exit point. Make sure you have good non-slip soles to your boots. Go with a friend. Never take risks on rocky headlands.*

including the *Lusitania*. The area offers just about every fish that swims the sea, including some very good blue shark fishing.

A little further west you come to the delightful village of Courtmacsherry, which has all the sea angler could want – along with a beautiful setting to boot. The reef fishing is superb, with some huge common skate in residence – fish to nearly 200 pounds have been caught. You can pick up conger from the pier, and mullet and tremendous bass and flounder off the beaches. It's a great place for the whole family – there's lots of exploring to be done and you can always have a bash at the mullet that throng the area around the pier. Try very small pieces of mackerel on a size ten, for example. You can actually watch the meat going down amongst them and free-line. Or you could use a small float. It's the sort of fishing that children adore.

ACCOMMODATION – try the Cork Tourist Information Centre on 00 353 (0)21 4273251.

TACKLE SHOPS – contact the Cobh Angling Centre in Cork on 00 353 (0)21 1813417 for tackle and for advice and contacts in the Cork area.

BOAT HIRE – ring the Cobh Angling Centre (see above). For information on blue shark fishing, contact the Castle Park Marina Centre on 00 353 (0)21 774959. Also try Mark Gannon in Courtmacsherry on 00 353 (0)23 46427; Mark is very much one of the local experts and offers both accommodation, charter-boat hire and unparalleled knowledge of the area.

CAHERSIVEEN

The south west is where everything really begins to take off. How about the little village of Cahersiveen in south-west Kerry? It's just north of the enchanting town of Waterville and is set in really beautiful countryside on the famous Ring of Kerry. It's an all-round sea-angling holiday destination. It's close to Valentia Island, but there is a myriad of small islands, rocks, jetties, harbours – perfect for shore fishing and boat fishing alike.

The boat fishing here is very well organised and productive. And there are lots of pollack to be caught close in. Cuckoo and ballan wrasse proliferate, along with plenty of mackerel. You'll find coley, ling, bull huss, haddock, cod, plaice and even skate and shark in the deeper water. What more could you possibly ask for? And if it's conger you fancy, try the pier after dark.

Shore fishing is brilliant. Fishing from the pier is great, but also try the road bridge and the old stone fort. Coonanna Harbour also offers a tremendous amount of opportunity for pollack, wrasse and dogfish. Check out the mullet and the very big bass. You will also find a lot of the shore fishing blissfully unexploited, as most of the locals tend to go out in boats. Be prepared to do a bit of exploring.

ACCOMMODATION – contact the Irish Tourist Board on 00 353 (0)20 74933201; they have an exhaustive list of accommodation in the area. Highly recommended is the Reenard House Bed and Breakfast on 00 353 (0)66 9472752 – a lovely place with great views.

TACKLE SHOPS AND BOAT HIRE – as far as the fishing goes, the Anchor Bar is the centre for everything that goes on – bar, tackle shop, meeting place and charter-boat hire centre! Hugh Maguire on 00 353 (0)66 9472049 can help with boat arrangements.

DINGLE AND TRALEE

Beautiful Dingle Bay can be found just to the north of Cahersiveen. One of the most popular places to fish from the shore here is Clogher Head, on the north side of the bay. To get there, follow the road out of Dingle for Smerwick Harbour. Drive through the village of Ballyferriter and carry on for a couple of miles. The cove is signposted. There's a headland about a mile away with a car-park overlooking the small beach. It's a really good rock-fishing venue, and the sandy cove itself can produce good sport at times. You'll pick up specimen wrasse and pollack from the rocks. There are also huss and conger eels. The sandy beach throws up flounder, dab, dogfish and plaice. It's a beautiful area, best fished from April through to October – fitting in nicely with the holiday season. Do take great care when you are fishing the rocks, and don't think of going down there if there's an onshore wind or a big swell – it could prove dangerous.

Moving up the coast again, we come to the popular Tralee Bay and the famous little fishing village of Fenit. Fenit is well sheltered, in common with many of the little ports in this fascinating part of the world. The boat fishing is spectacular. June to September is tremendous for skate and the shallow water inside Tralee Bay offers marvellous fishing for both tope and monkfish. May and June are peak times. It's common to use a rubby bag and a mackerel flapper as bait. If the wind is kind, you can travel far out, but if it's stormy, you can just tuck into the bay itself and enjoy some cracking sport there. The shore fishing is also superb. Monkfish are possible and the bass fishing is excellent. You can even, if you're lucky, pick up common skate from the pier! So if boat fishing isn't for you, there are other possibilities!

ACCOMMODATION – in Dingle, contact the Tourist Information Centre on 00 353 (0)62 61333 or try the Pax House on 00 353 (0)66 9151518. In Tralee, contact the Tourist Information Centre on 00 353 (0)66 21288 or try the Rosedale Lodge on 00 353 (0)66 7125320. In Fenit, Godley's Hotel is the centre for everything – you can contact them on 00 353 (0)66 36108.

TACKLE SHOPS – tackle can be bought at the Dingle Marina (see below).

BOAT HIRE – contact the Dingle Marina on 00 353 (0)66 59947.

KILRUSH

The Shannon estuary has some great possibilities, and the town of Kilrush is particularly popular. There's some superb pier fishing offering conger, flounder and dogfish. However, the shark-fishing possibilities are enormous and so it pays to consider getting afloat.

Kilrush certainly merits the support of sea anglers everywhere. Several million pounds have been spent on creating a lock system to trap the flow of the Shannon and to give access from the spanking new marina out onto the sea. What you have now at Kilrush is a safe base – even in the winter – on the exposed west coast of Ireland, along with the security and the facilities of a purpose-built marina.

The fishing is absolutely superb. There are plenty of tope, which provide great sport on lighter gear. Thornbacks proliferate, along with bull huss, common skate, conger and blue shark. There are endless well-known marks such as Scattery Island and Carrigaholt Bay. Excellent stuff.

⊨ **ACCOMMODATION** – Shannon Angling on 00 353 (0)65 52031 offers both boat charter and accommodation.

○ **TACKLE SHOPS** – contact Michael O'Sullivan on 00 353 (0)65 51071 or Michael Clancy on 00 353 (0)65 51107.

➥ **BOAT HIRE** – try Atlantic Adventures on 00 353 (0)65 52133 or Shannon Angling (as above). The Kilrush Creek Marina on 00 353 (0)65 52072 is the hub of everything.

CONNEMARA

Moving up to Connemara, you can't do better than the town of Clifden – really picturesque, great bars, great scenery and some great fishing. There are really good possibilities for deep-sea shark fishing. Another excellent place is Westport, in the south-east corner of the famous Clew Bay. Clew Bay is sheltered by the wonderful Achill and Clare Islands. This is a huge bay dotted with some 300 tiny islands, so there's always shelter for those wanting to take a boat out.

The fishing is quite magnificent. Inside Clew Bay, you'll find ray, tope, skate and turbot. Move a little out of the bay and you'll come into the grounds of cod, pollack, coalfish and the occasional John Dory. You've got to go heavy for the skate hereabouts because they really grow large – it's wise to use fifty- to eighty-pound plus gear, with perhaps 8/0 hooks. Remember that it's illegal to kill skate and all must be tagged and returned. You can go a bit lighter for the tope fishing – thirty-pound class should suffice, with 6/0 hooks. You'll need a wire trace and a long leader of very heavy nylon. If tope begin to twist, then lighter lines can go with a vengeance.

FISHING FOR TOPE

Tope are a free-running species, so you will get a tremendous all-action fight from them. Ireland is one of the really hot areas for tope fishing.

• *When you are fishing over a rugged reef or a place where there are snags or very strong currents, thirty- or even fifty-pound class tackle is advisable.*

• *If the water is shallow and sandy without big tidal pushes, very heavy freshwater gear will mostly suffice. Use heavy carp or pike rods, along with fifteen- or twenty-pound line.*

• *Mono is generally considered preferable to braid for tope fishing. The elasticity of mono, often considered a drawback in many forms of sea fishing, is actually good when you're pursuing very fast-swimming tope. Line stretch is often a blessing, especially for the inexperienced angler.*

• *Rigs: you needn't use more than twelve to eighteen inches of wire to cope with a tope's teeth. A few feet of heavy-duty nylon – sixty to 100 pounds – make up the leader. Hooks should be 6/0 or 8/0, depending on bait.*

• *Bait: a whole dead mackerel can produce big fish, but also use strips of the fish and try and leave the guts exposed. Cut off the tail of any dead fish to stop it twisting in the tide, looking suspicious and kinking the line. Calamari squid provide a really good alternative bait.*

• *Timing the strike: tope have often been thought of much like pike – they run, stop, turn the bait and then take it in. For this reason, tope angling in the past was often built around the longest delayed strike. This resulted in deep hooking and dead fish. Far better to hit a fish soon after the run develops. Timing is largely down to experience. Strike early with the first run and, if you miss, just delay a few seconds for the next and so on. A lost fish is better than a deeply hooked dead one.*

• *Play the fish calmly and with determination. Don't let the tope dominate the fight or it will simply tire itself out.*

• *Once in the boat, don't let a tope thrash about on the bottom. A carp-style unhooking mat is a very good idea here for the fish's welfare. Try to kneel over the fish so that it's between your legs – it's head, obviously, pointing away from you. A T-bar disgorger is necessary to get beyond the teeth and to have enough grip to get the hook from the tough skin. Try to have somebody else keeping control of the tail.*

• *If you must take a photograph, make sure that you support the weight of its body cavity with your arm to avoid damaging the fish internally.*

• *Above all, get that fish back as quickly as possible. Tope are coming back big time; only our care for them will see this promising trend continue.*

Check out Tramore Bay, not a particularly well-marked place, but one that offers fantastic tope fishing, especially around Claggan Island. Tramore is attractive to tope because of the huge numbers of flatfish it contains. There are also mussel beds to the west, home to giant monkfish. Multiple catches of tope around Claggan Island are not unusual, with some big fish amongst them. The Central Fisheries Board has had a tagging operation in place for some time now, and catch and release is certainly the way forward.

This is excellent sport – the water is shallow and often clear with endless inlets and bays to explore. And in such skinny water, don't the fish go! Expect long runs and breathtaking fights, especially on light gear.

This part of Eire is now easily accessible. Of course, you can still do the mammoth drive across England, ferry cross the Irish Sea and then drive the breadth of Ireland. Alternatively, you can fly into Knock Airport in no time at all.

⊨ ACCOMMODATION – for angler-friendly accommodation, contact Josephine and Mattie Geraghty on 00 353 (0)97 85741.

⚓ BOAT HIRE – the area is well set up with enterprising skippers. Try Micky Lavelle on 00 353 (0)97 85669. For deep-sea shark fishing, contact J. Brittain on 00 353 (0)95 21073 or J. Ryan on 00 353 (0)95 21069.

DONEGAL

Let's move north even further, up to the splendid county of Donegal. Downings is really beginning to make a reputation for itself, just inland from the famous Tory Island. There's tremendous shore fishing around here, with piers, rocks, estuaries and beaches. The pier offers conger, especially on a mackerel head at night. You'll also find flounder, plaice and dab. If you move westwards from the pier, you'll come across several rock marks. Expect thornback, ray, flatfish, pollack and mackerel – superb spinning opportunities during the summer months.

Close by is the wonderful beach of Tra Na Rossan. This offers brilliant September and early October opportunities with bass. Try to the left of the beach, tight to the rocks – especially on the early flood tide. You'll pick up flatfish all the year, with plaice quite common from June through to October. Also expect thornback and spotted ray and a few turbot in the early autumn. Huss come close into those rocks at night.

Going back to Downings, it would be totally wrong not to mention the most exciting development of all, one that has all tongues wagging – the return of the blue-fin tuna, the so called 'tunny' that dominated the big game-fishing psyche back in the 1930s and 1940s. In those days, most of the fishing took place on the east coast of England, but the overfishing of mackerel shoals drove these monstrous, beautiful creatures away. Nowadays, however, there are signs that the coast of Donegal could be the new stamping ground for people wishing to test themselves against these spectacular fish.

Much of this has to do with the North Atlantic drift, which warms the coastal waters as it brushes the west coast of Ireland on its way to Scotland. The big fish follow their prey and come close in to the coast of Donegal. Mid-August is, arguably, the best time of all but the season does run much earlier and later. You're talking about big fish – certainly 300- and 400-pounders, but tuna of 500 to 1,000 pounds are always possible. For this reason, you must use heavy-duty gear. We're talking a 130-pound test with 16/0 hooks allied with 300- or even 400-pound traces. These fish battle brutally: they'll pick up your mackerel bait with a screaming run and then give a wonderful fight. They run long and hard, always pushing deeper. Okay, you won't see them tail-walking, but that doesn't take anything from the wonder of the fight. These are fish that just never give in.

What you don't really want – for your comfort as much as anything else – is stormy weather. You will often find these massive fish pretty close in, certainly within four or five miles of the shore. The mackerel are the key to finding them, being the major prey of the tuna shoals. Of course, you're never quite sure at what level the mackerel are running and where the fish will be feeding, though on some blessed occasions you will actually see the tuna hit into shoals of mackerel on the surface. Could there be a more exciting sight on the seas?

It's most common to use balloons as floats and set your baits – live mackerel – at differing depths. For example, work some on the surface, others at mid-water and others down deep, just off the bottom, in fact. A preferred method is to use a live mackerel and troll it very slowly behind the boat. Be warned, you'll be in no doubt when a tuna is on – prepare for absolute fireworks.

Derek Noble is really the expert on tuna fishing in Ireland. He reckons that late August through to October is the very best time for these amazing fish. They probably hang on later than that, but weather, of course, is a major problem. It's taken Derek quite a long time to get to grips with the fish and, even though he was seeing them, it was a while before he began to experience hook-ups. Live mackerel are good, but artificials also can work well when, like Derek, you know what you're doing.

There's certainly no shortage of fish. Some of the groups are only five or six strong, but thirty to forty is probably more common. And, just occasionally, you will see hundreds, with areas of water twice the size of a

139

football pitch just erupting with these big fish – and I mean big. The average size of the tuna that Derek is taking at the moment is something over 300 pounds – and that's nothing! In September 2001, he saw a colossal fish come out of the water about seventy yards away from his boat – a fish well over 400 pounds. This is really thrilling stuff and you don't necessarily have to hook into a fish to appreciate the day if you see one as close as this. As Derek says, to watch the sea-birds shear off the surface as these colossal fish plough through the waves is a sight never to be forgotten.

One thing that Derek stresses is a catch-and-release policy. It's important to be seen to be doing our bit for the future and although tuna can be valuable, it has to be taken in and iced as quickly as possible – not something you want to do if you're intent on enjoying a day's sport. So, put the monetary side right out of your mind and just enjoy one of the most incredible sport-fishing experiences in the world today. And it's virtually on our doorstep!

ACCOMMODATION – contact the Tourist Information Office on 00 353 (0)7161201.

TACKLE SHOPS – try Erinn Tackle in nearby Ramelton on 00 353 (0)87639 3933 for all the latest information.

BOAT HIRE – contact E. O'Callaghan on 00 353 (0)7331288, Brian McGilloway on 00 353 (0)7331144 or Antony Doherty on 00 353 (0)7331079.

PORTRUSH AND RATHLIN ISLAND

The availability of sea fishing in Northern Ireland has been promoted on a huge scale over the last few years. The Northern Irish Tourist Board has recognised that angling is a very important part of tourism in Ireland and has worked diligently to promote it. With excellent results, too, – both on the fresh- and sea-water fronts. Southern Ireland often grabs the attention when it comes to all manner of fishing, but the north shouldn't be forgotten – certainly for sea fish. It boasts hundreds of miles of staggeringly beautiful coastline, unpolluted and unexploited. There are well over twenty species of sea fish regularly caught, including all the favourites such as bass, tope, shark and skate.

Portrush is a favourite area near the mouth of Lough Foyle and the River Bann. The town offers good pier and beach fishing and there are conger in the harbour itself.

Moving round the coast, we come to the magical Rathlin Island, situated a little way off the coast opposite the town of Ballycastle. This offers really good wreck fishing in Church Bay and some tremendous sport with just about everything.

BRAID

As technology moves on, braid becomes ever more efficient, offering an alternative to nylon. It is perfect for signalling bites... the slightest tap bucks the rod over. With its reduced diameter it's excellent for holding deep water in strong tides with a minimum of lead. It's also limp and doesn't spook the fish, but there can be problems.

• *Knots and braid haven't always gone well together, so obey any knotting instructions that come with the line. Use a doubled length of line for all knots. Dab superglue on the knots for added strength.*

• *Put the backing on the reel as tight as it will go to avoid bedding-in. Load the braid itself under pressure and not just from a free spool. This will probably require a friend to help out.*

• *Casting is easy with a fixed-spool reel, but not as straightforward with a multiplier. Presuming you are using a multiplier, don't go too fine or the spool's braking will cause a problem. If this is proving difficult consider using the new forms of coated braid, which can help.*

• *Start your cast with maximum braking force – for example, two big brake locks and the use of thick oil. Make sure your cast is smooth and not snatched.*

• *Use a longer shock leader than usual – say ten or twelve turns round the spool, at least.*

• *Braid comes into its own particularly when spinning or float fishing with a delicate rod and fixed-spool reel. Casting is enhanced, and there is less chance of breaking up on fine lines.*

• *Always check your braid very carefully for any evidence of wear and tear. It might seem indestructible, and often proves to be so when you're pulling for a break, however, when you go to unhook that elusive monster conger it can snap like cotton! If you're in any doubt, and you fear that the line may be fraying, then, expensive though it may be, re-spool and start again.*

• *My own opinion? I'm going to be controversial here: experience in many different types of water all over the world leads me to say that if you are fishing over particularly rocky and punishing ground then you are possibly better off considering ordinary nylon. In my experience, nylon is that little bit more resistant to the chafing that harsh ground gives it and is less likely to snap unexpectedly. Braid does have many advantages, but the measure of unpredictability in tough environments casts doubt over it in my mind.*

ACCOMMODATION – contact the Tourist Information Centre in Portrush on 028 7082 3333.

TACKLE SHOPS – Joe Mullan is a mine of information; contact him at his tackle shop at 74 Main Street, Portrush.

BOAT HIRE – Geoff Farrow in Portstewart (close to Portrush) offers boats for hire – contact him on 01265 836622. Contact C. McCaughan on 01265 762074 for details about boats in the Rathlin Island area.

BANGOR AND DONAGHADEE

Just over ten miles from Belfast city itself, you'll find the town of Bangor situated on Belfast Lough. This lough offers some really sheltered, prolific fishing. You can dig your own lugworm and expect to catch good flatfish, along with codling and whiting in season. There are even some turbot.

Just south of Bangor, you will come to Donaghadee, which offers pier and rock fishing for pollack and codling and huge numbers of mackerel in the summer months. The Rigg sandbar is a good mark off shore, offering mixed sport.

ACCOMMODATION – contact the Tourist Information Centre in Bangor on 028 9127 0069.

TACKLE SHOPS – try Trap and Tackle on 01247 458515.

BOAT HIRE – contact Mr Nelson on 01247 883403 for wreck and reef fishing.

STRANGFORD LOUGH

Strangford Lough offers some superb boat fishing and is sheltered from all but the very worst of the winds. There's excellent skate and tope fishing, but note that both fish are protected and must be returned alive. There's some very good wrasse around the entrance to the lough where the water is deep.

One of the beauties of sea fishing in Northern Ireland is that, to some extent, you are still, even in the 21st century, something of a pioneer. Okay, the locals and some visitors in the know are well aware of the possibilities but even today the vast majority of visiting anglers still head for the south. This can be a mistake when you consider the big opportunities and the warm welcome that the north extends.

ACCOMMODATION – contact the Tourist Information Centre in Bangor on 028 9127 0069.

TACKLE SHOPS – contact Country Sports at nearby Newtownards on 01247 812585.

BOAT HIRE – charter boats are available in the nearby town of Portaferry – contact Mr Rogers on 01247 728297 for details.

AUTHOR'S ACKNOWLEDGEMENTS

So many people have helped me with this book that it's hard to know where to begin, but particular mention must be made of Bernard Bishop and, indeed, all his family who have helped me so much, in so many ways, for so many years up here in Norfolk.

Thanks to Robin Armstrong for all his tips on South-West England and for all his years of friendship. Thank you to Richie Johnston – I can never think of Ireland without mulling over your hospitality and that of David and Charlie, too. My affection for Peter Smith is unbounded and I've always found his help limitless.

Thank you also to Terry Thomas, Andy Nicholson, Bob Moss and Keith Elliott – four great blokes and men whose fishing ability always leaves me breathless. Thank you especially to Jan Porter at Shimano for all his help with rods… believe me, those uptiders are quite exceptional, even for mahseer out in India.

Thank you Clive Gammon – what an inspiration you've been. Thanks, also, to Christopher West – life would have been much more empty without knowing you. Thank you to Carol who, as usual, has kept me sane throughout this arduous enterprise.

Above all, thank you to Jim Whippy. Jim, as you're quite aware, I couldn't even have contemplated doing this without your help and excellent photos.